Ex Libris

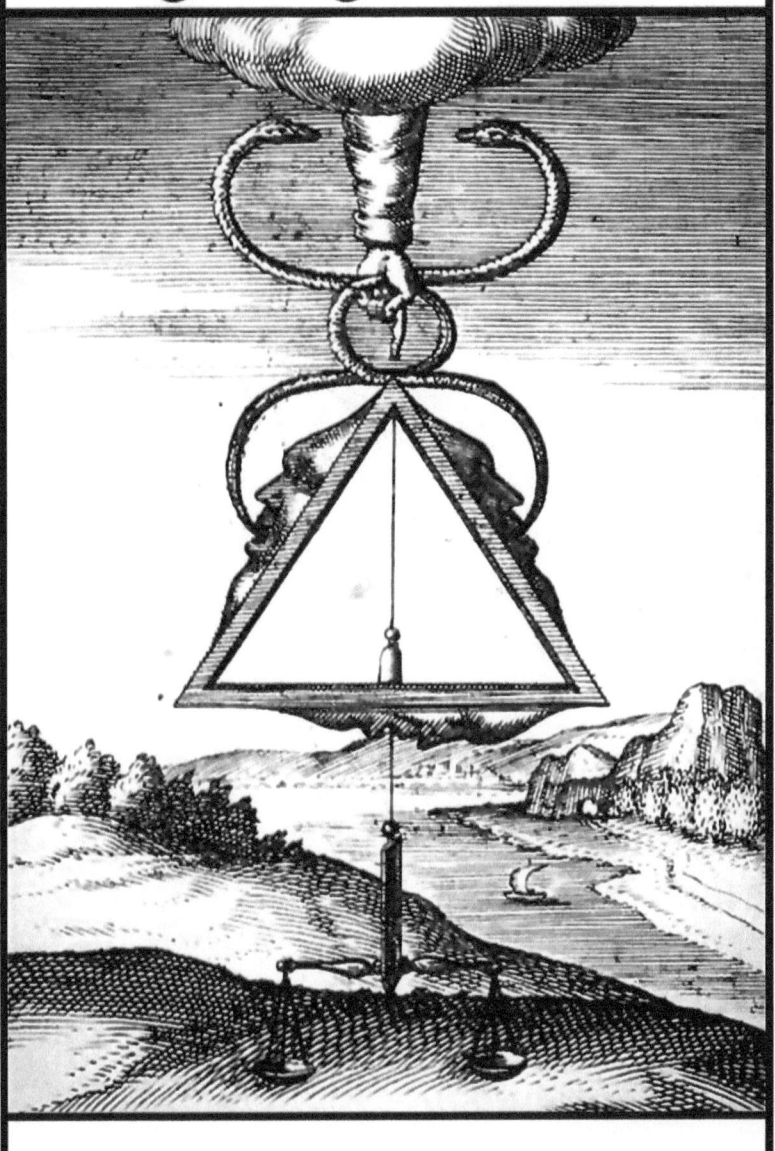

Kindest regards of
Manly P. Hall

Manly P. Hall, Illustration by Jessica Naomi

Manly P. Hall A Seeker of More Intelligent Life – Book Second

Compiled with graphics and edits by Darrell Jordan, Copyright © First Edition 2023. All rights reserved.

No part of this book may be reproduced in whole or in part without the written permission from the publisher, nor stored in any retrieval system or transmitted by any means, electronic, mechanical, photocopying, recording, or other, without the written consent of the publisher.

For bulk purchases, please contact the publisher.

Enquiry@Athenaia.Co

Library of Congress Cataloging-in Publication Data

Names: Hall, Manly P. | Jordan, Darrell

Title: Manly P. Hall A Seeker of More Intelligent Life – Book Second

Description: First U.S. edition. | Coeur D'Alene, Idaho: Athenaia [2023]

Identifiers: LCCN (pending) | ISBN 979-8-88556-044-3 (First Edition hardcover)

Subjects: OCC040000: BODY, MIND & SPIRIT / Hermetism & Rosicrucianism, | PHI013000: PHILOSOPHY / Metaphysics, | SOC038000: SOCIAL SCIENCE / Freemasonry & Secret Societies

LC record available at https://lccn. loc.go

On the internet: Parallel47North.com/collections/esoteric-books

Managing Editor: Darrell Jordan

Original Author and Essay: Manly P. Hall

Executive Producer: Yuka Jordan

Book Cover Art and Illustrations: Jessica Naomi

Image Credits: Manly P. Hall's personal collection

Printed and bound in the United States

Publisher: Athenaia, LLC

2370 N Merritt Crk Lp, Ste 1

Coeur D'Alene, ID 83814

The United States

Manly P. Hall

A Seeker of More Intelligent Life

Book Second

Darrell Jordan, MPS

CONTENTS

INTRODUCTION	9
WASHINGTON D.C., MAY 1, 1935	11
LOS ANGELES, CALF. JUNE 1, 1935	24
QUESTIONS AND ANSWERS	30
LOS ANGELES, JULY 1, 1935	36
LOS ANGELES, AUGUST 1, 1935	48
QUESTIONS AND ANSWERS	55
LOS ANGELES, SEPTEMBER 1, 1935	61
LOS ANGELES, OCTOBER 1, 1935	73
LOS ANGELES, NOVEMBER 1, 1935	86
QUESTIONS AND ANSWERS	93
LOS ANGELES, CALF. DECEMBER 1, 1935	99
QUESTIONS AND ANSWERS	106
LOS ANGELES, CALF. JANUARY 1, 1936	112
QUESTIONS AND ANSWERS	119
LOS ANGELES, FEBRUARY 1, 1936	124
MARCH 1, 1936	137
QUESTIONS AND ANSWERS	143
SPECIAL ARTICLES	149
APRIL 1, 1936	149
AUTHOR AND MANAGING EDITOR	163
MANLY P. HALL BOOK SERIES	165

INTRODUCTION

EDITOR'S NOTE

Manley Hall was born on 18 March 1901, in Peterborough, Canada, to William S. and Louise Palmer Hall. The Hall family moved to Sioux Falls, South Dakota, United States, in 1904. Manly Hall later settled in Los Angeles in 1919.

As a young man, he became interested in all forms of occult subjects. He subsequently joined a number of societies, among them the Theosophical Society, the Freemasons, the Societas Rosecruciana in Civitatibus Foederatis, and the American Federation of Astrologers.

In 1922, Hall wrote his first book: Initiates of the Flame and was collecting all form of esoteric/exoteric/mystical subject matter, in his own words: "late in the fall of 1922, the plan for a comprehensive work on the symbolism of western mystical societies began to take shape in my mind. It soon became apparent that research facilities for such a project were not available in Southern California... The only answer was to contact antiquarian book dealers and elicit their cooperation in the search for the items desired." In 1934, Hall founded the Philosophical Research Society, a research institute modeled on the ancient school of Pythagoras.

He was ordained a minister in 1923 to an occult/mystic congregation at the Church of the People in California. In that same year specifically in May 1923, Manly Hall began the membership/student based, not for sale magazine, all written, edited and published by Hall titled the "The All Seeing-Eye."

We now follow Manly P. Hall from the "All Seeing Eye" book series at the age of 24, to his private lessons for his students in this latest book series, at the age of 32. In this series, Mr. Hall moves from imparting wisdom through stories to a confident, fact-based approach of his findings and understanding of his research. His elucidation exudes confidence and is well written, with it being exceedingly broad in scope. In this series we provide 4 years of lessons condensed into four books. We are positive you will find the information herein to be quite useful in filling in some hidden areas of understanding in religion and history.

Editing was minimal in terms of punctuation and spelling. In some cases, there are made-up words (or words that are no longer in use) in which case they were left spelled as is.

I'm sure that you will find, as did I, that Manly Hall was highly intelligent and possibly bordering on genius. Suffice it to say, we are positive you will enjoy the many journeys Manly Hall takes you on.

Darrell Jordan, MPS

WASHINGTON D.C., MAY 1, 1935

Dear Friend,

The second year of our Student's Monthly Letter begins with this issue. We feel that many people studying the Ancient Wisdom teachings will be interested in a more or less detailed consideration of vital problems which arise in the course of their studies. The pursuit of knowledge is beset with numerous hazards. Questions arise, problems present themselves, and the course of action becomes confused and tangled. In order that the mind may be left free in its quest for essential truth, there must be a general sense of intellectual security. Benjamin Franklin is accredited with the adage: "Be sure you are right and then go ahead." In devoting our next twelve letters to vital questions dealing with metaphysical issues we hope to correct some popular misconceptions in the field and assist the average student to orient himself in the vast world of philosophy. Each month, therefore, we will take some major problem and after treating its general significance break it up into its lesser aspects and indicate a sound course of action in the department of thinking or living under consideration.

QUESTION:

How can a student of the ancient wisdom teachings contact bona fide sources of occult philosophy and spiritual instruction? What is the safest course for students of higher knowledge to pursue at this time in their quest for wisdom?

ANSWER:

For thousands of years, the wisest and noblest of human beings in every civilization and nation have desired truth above any temporal position. The quest for truth is life's noblest adventure, and the achievement of truth is the perfect reward for perfect action. There is a well-worn path which Buddha called the Middle Way which avoids all of the extremes and inconsistencies of action and leads finally to a life of wisdom. Thousands of years of experience have established and developed, and to a relative degree perfected, the science of salvation through wisdom. There is one right way and many wrong ways to do anything. There is only one entrance to the great temple of universal knowledge. He who attempts to go in by any other door or to storm the high citadel of truth, the same is a "thief and a robber." Those who dedicate themselves to the processes of discipline and self-improvement set down by the old masters are preparing themselves, to enter the house of wisdom by the proper gate. On the other hand, such foolish mortals as believe they can breathe, chant, intone, psychologize or affirm themselves into a state of all-knowing are trying to pick locks for which they have not filed the key—Such misguided ones are like the howling dervishes described by Omar who wail before the temple gates but have nothing in them that merits their admission.

As Immanuel Kant has pointed out, man searching for wisdom has two courses open to him. He may either direct his faculties inwardly to achieve an internal contact with the source of wisdom, or he may direct his attention outwardly in an effort to know through an external contact with the phenomena of existence. In simpler terms, he can search for truth either inside or outside of himself. Truth from within or from Self may be termed inspiration, and truth from without, from other persons or things, may be termed instruction. Truth, either as inspiration or instruction, when applied, becomes experience. We may define experience as the test of action, and by experiencing man makes universal wisdom his own.

We will first consider the problem of inspiration or wisdom arising from internal contact. It is theoretically evident that this approach has its hazards, as well as its advantages, and in practice these hazards in most cases assume formidable proportions. The three chief advantages of the inspirational approach are:

1st: Knowledge from within is unadulterated by opinion and interpretation, nor has it been subjected to the devitalizing influence of sectarianism.

2nd: Knowledge from within binds the student more closely to the source of wisdom, creating a state of mental and spiritual sufficiency not dependent upon the hazardous props of organized religion. Each man and the God within him constitute a majority.

3rd: Inspirational knowledge is always to a great degree attuned to the need of the individual who receives it. An inspiration does not flow into a consciousness utterly unfit to receive it. There is, therefore, a practicability and a reasonableness of relationship between inspiration and the one inspired.

To summarize, therefore, we may say that inspiration is a relationship with universal truth much to be desired and the end towards which all learning must eventually lead. Unfortunately, the course of inspirational knowing is beset with certain distinct hazards which are painfully evident among modern metaphysicians. To understand these hazards, it is necessary to examine briefly certain aspects of the subjective life of man—his psychical anatomy and physiology, as it were. If man consisted only of spirit and body, inspirationalism would offer no difficulties, but unhappily for the average mystic there intervenes between consciousness and form a considerable array of psychical impulses and forces. There is a psychical organism which is the power behind our sensory and emotional reflexes, and in the practice of mysticism these psychical equations often confuse the issues of inspiration. A man who believes that he has just received a direct message from the Infinite may be only getting a reflex from some psychological complex, reflex or inhibition which he is carrying about with him in his subconscious or subjective personality. As long as the human soul remains a tangle of instincts, appetites, antipathies and attachments, as it is with the average person, only a very wise man can isolate and identify a true inspiration.

From this, it should be evident that inspiration is not a substitute for philosophical discipline. It is only after the individual has well organized his whole life, by self-control and the rationalizing of all his perceptions, that he is really capable of measuring the merits and demerits of so-called inspirational flashes and revelations. The major hazards of inspirationalism and the various systems of metaphysical "absolutism" can be collected for practical purposes under three headings:

1st: It is almost impossible for the average person, even after many years of metaphysical study, to accurately determine the difference between inspiration and imagination. What may at first appear to be the very staff of truth may prove in time to be merely the substance of things hoped for.

2nd: The impossibility of determining with certainty the real source and substance of a presumed inspiration very often leaves the student a victim to the most grotesque absurdities of his own subconscious mind.

3rd: As efforts to develop the inspirational faculties are usually desultory, unscientific, and have about them much of a philosophy of self-negation, these efforts frequently lead to mediumship or even obsession. Under such conditions the source of the supposed inspiration may be an obsessing or possessing entity utterly unqualified to regulate the affairs of the earnest seeker. In substance then, while the true Self is beyond doubt the perfect teacher and the source of all eternal good, the way to that Self is so beset with snares, pitfalls and illusions that the novice cannot safely attempt this path until noble motive is supported by sufficient knowledge and a high measure of discrimination.

In this matter, we speak from a wealth of experience. Scarcely a week goes by but some earnest and benighted soul brings to us a story of "cosmic revelation." Most of these people have left some orthodox faith behind them and are shipwrecked in a sea of notions. These poor folk bring their visions, intuitions, and psychical experiences to us for confirmation. If we point out the absurdity of that which is evidently absurd, we, of course, incur the displeasure of these people who feel that we have no right to question the validity of what to them is a real "inward experience."

It is useless to explain that "inward" is a very large term covering not only man's spiritual part but also his whole psychical organism, and to be exactly literal also his stomach and liver. In contacting hundreds of people obsessed by the significance of their "inward" experiences or visions, I have never yet found a case of real inspiration or spiritual vision apart from a well-organized, well-informed mind, well balanced and normally manifested emotions, and a high state of spiritual and intellectual superiority. Neurotic, inhibited people may have psychical experiences, and occasionally some of their visions may have a small personal fulfillment. The real philosopher, however, is not interested in Ouija-boards even if occasionally they tell the truth. An acceptable quality of inspiration must transcend small phenomenal problems.

The monks of Zen Buddhism, whose whole doctrine is one of internal truth, have left us some good precepts. They say that when a man talks with his Real Self, when through the highest of human accomplishments, he is lifted up to that truth ever-abiding within him, he neither sees nor hears anything. No elaborate or fantastic visions come to him, nor do beings of the invisible world deliver vast orations. The little self (personality), when elevated to temporary identity with the great Self (universality), neither senses nor perceives, but rather—KNOWS. For that which is known under such conditions, there is no word.

He who possesses truth can neither describe nor define it but, momentarily becoming it, has a complete sense of participation in it. This highest wisdom is a silent fact. Those who achieve to it in silence, preserve it in silence, and teach it in silence. Man can be instructed by word and act as to the way of accomplishment, but concerning the accomplishment itself, all of the great teachings are alike—silent.

* * * * *

From the first approach to truth, that of internal contact, we shall now turn to the second, the path of external contact. It should be understood that truth itself is superior to any of the means by which we try to achieve it. All progress leads towards truth. Progress, growth and development are manifestations of the impulse towards truth, but the means should never be confused with the end. When we refer, therefore, to the achievement of truth by external contact, we do not mean that Reality itself is to be perceived outwardly, but rather that from certain outward contacts we may gain instruments of comprehension and understanding by which we are better fitted to approach the mystery of truth itself.

We shall now consider mediums of external contact or instruction in mystical matters under three headings:

1st: Institutions or individuals claiming to possess an exact knowledge of the disciplines by which man may be elevated to a condition of spiritual security.

2nd: The literature of the ages, including religious and philosophical books supposed to contain knowledge sufficient to enable the student to gain a solid foundation in the metaphysical sciences.

3rd: Nature itself with its numerous examples of spiritual processes, and all forms of example, action and reaction, through the observation of which a student may gain a reasonable education in universal law.

These three external paths to wisdom are a development of Buddha's Three Jewels, or as he termed them: The Life, the Word, and the Church, by which the tradition is perpetuated. By the church we are to understand all spiritual organizations. By the word, the world's vast literature of wisdom. By the life, nature itself and the example of truth in action. These three media which exist in the material universe as means to the achievement of truth indicate the three steps of the philosophical temple which must inevitably be climbed by each truth-seeker. In the school of philosophy, the lowest grade of novices is termed studentship, and this corresponds to the philosophy of action, and its word observation. They are stewards in the temple of nature. The second grade is that of discipleship. They must achieve their knowledge through study and experience. The third grade is made up of the initiates themselves and they represent the secret orders and schools by which the tradition is perpetuated in an organized manner. These three grades are another interpretation of Buddha's Three Jewels. The analogy is evident.

In our quest for sources of spiritual knowledge, we must now examine in more detail the three avenues of external contact or instruction. We will consider institutions and individuals claiming at the present time to be perpetuating the ageless tradition. Let us first examine institutions:

From the most ancient times colleges, schools, temples and communities devoted to the study and dissemination of the spiritual sciences have flourished among men. Although the schools of philosophy established by the Greeks, Egyptians, Romans and Chaldeans vanished with the passing of these civilizations, similar centers of culture have continued in Asia even to this present time. There is ample proof in the writings of the world's most illumined thinkers that distinct spiritual benefit was to be derived from participation in the teachings and disciplines of these sects and societies. The state Mysteries of the Greeks and the great ceremonial institutions of the Egyptians perpetuated the most obscure knowledge and bestowed upon qualified candidates the accumulated arcana of the race. If then, we may seem to criticize modern metaphysical organizations, it is not because we would depreciate the theory of philosophical societies, but rather because most modern orders have departed from the old footings and foundations and cannot be regarded as bona fide representatives of the older systems.

The important difference between ancient occult institutions and modern metaphysical societies may be considered under three headings:

1st: The great philosophical Mystery Schools of antiquity were administered by the state, whereas all modern organizations in the Western world are under private direction. This particular issue is more important than may first appear. Private organizations, struggling for existence, do not enjoy the security, authority or recognition necessary to a wide sphere of influence. A doctrine, which to be useful must be unified, is broken up into numberless relatively isolated fragments which can only exist by proselyting and competing one with the other. Where there are many sects, there is little wisdom. The old Mystery Schools were not reduced to the dilemma of maintaining themselves through high-pressure advertising and salesmanship, nor did financial necessity force them to accept into their rank's persons possessing none of the actual attributes qualifying them to receive spiritual instruction. The ancient world functioned in the consciousness of quality, while the modern world seeks to perpetuate itself on the theory of quantity alone. When we hear of a religious order that has a million members, or some philosophical society with several thousand "initiates," we are forced to the inevitable conclusion that the membership of the organization is bloated by a large contingency whose only active junction is dues-paying.

The ancient wisdom temples accepted only the best of men. Modern societies are forced, often against their own good judgement, to accept whoever fulfills the monetary requirement.

2nd: The instituted Mysteries of antiquity possessed an unbroken metaphysical tradition which had descended through a long line of hierophants from the dim beginnings of time. The merit of these systems can best be inferred by the high order of men and women who testified to the sublimity of the teaching. Pythagoras, Plato, Aristotle, Plutarch, Proclus, Plotinus, Hypatia, Phidias, Hippocrates, Cicero and a host of others acknowledged the supremacy of the instituted Mysteries of the Greeks or Romans. Minds of this quality are not easily deluded by superficial doctrines. Orders which gained the admiration of such intellects must indeed have been admirable throughout. Most modern mystical societies are orders of quest and not orders of achievement. They are based upon the opinions and interpretations of individuals and not upon any collected body of learning. Hundreds of little sects spring up and gather small groups of earnest followers about them. Soon contentions and contriving's set in and these sects collapse into themselves and are heard of no more. Old experienced "joiners" of modern mystical movements are for the most part a disillusioned lot.

3rd: Institutions like the Mystery temples of antiquity cannot flourish in a social order, essentially contrary to their principles. The state Mysteries of the older nations were part of the spirit of their time. Men, regarding wisdom as the chief of the virtues and not dominated by a vicious economic complex, respected their centers of learning and gave a large measure of moral support to these most prized of their institutions. Modern occult movements, drawing their membership from a commercialized, materialized and essentially selfish social order, are bound to be corrupted and finally dissipated by the character tendencies of their own members. A man can bring to a system of thought only what he is and when many selfish persons gather to support an unselfish cause, it is the common end that this unselfish cause gradually dies out, drowned in a sea of selfishness. When two or more are gathered together in this modern world, self-interest is almost bound to be present also. Self-interest is fatal to the common good, and politics has no place in the house of truth.

The path of organized mysticism in the modern world is therefore beset with many troubles, and persons associating themselves with modern societies are very apt to gain more exasperation than inspiration from their affiliations.

We should next examine existing occult movements by classifying them under two general headings which we will term simply sincere and insincere. This particular issue has nothing to do with the antiquity of the movement or its presumed relationships with older organizations. It simply is concerned with the question: Is the movement honest or dishonest? Of course, it is not within the province of our treatment to refer to specific organizations or to list the names of those which we believe to be honest or dishonest. We must concern ourselves only with principles and not become confused with the much less important element of personalities.

We consider those movements sincere which have the improvement of man as the real reason for their existence, and we regard those as insincere and utterly despicable which are dedicated to profit and are exploiting for their own gain the spiritual aspirations of honest men and women.

It does not necessarily follow that even a sincere organization can completely neglect its financial problems. As long as philosophical movements are not supported by the state, they must be supported by the intelligent cooperation of their members. To be worthy of confidence a philosophical organization must indicate that it is capable of honestly and constructively administering its finances. On the other hand, nearly all religious and philosophical institutions of the Western world are incorporated as non-profit corporations. They must be supported and they must demand a reasonable measure of support, but when they enter into the field of exploitation and misrepresentation for profit, they forfeit the respect and support of all sincere students.

Students of a mind to affiliate with an occult organization should examine with the greatest of care the merits and demerits of the movement. It is the height of folly to impulsively link oneself with any organization which has not been thoroughly examined and analyzed with all discrimination. Fantastically named organizations with glamorous pretensions and impossible presumptions should, of course, be entirely avoided. Any group claiming to be the only possessors of most ancient and profound secrets should be avoided at all costs. Simple, studious groups of intelligent men and women, making no pretensions but doing and living a high standard of personal and collective integrity, without fads or fetishes, and with no elaborate political machinery, are the only groups worthy of even passing consideration. There is no question but that such groups exist, but they seldom publicize themselves. Functioning quietly, they are known by their works and not by their words. To the "joiner," one passing thought: Weigh all things, and cling only to that which is simple, good, reasonable and honest.

From the claims of modern organizations as sources of spiritual education, we must now pass to the claims of individuals presuming to be ambassadors of secret systems of knowledge. At the present time fraud in this field is particularly flagrant. Taken all together, individual teachers are a more hazardous problem than organizations. The latter have a certain physical tangibility about them and their claims are more easily checked, proved or disproved. The itinerant teacher, on the other hand, must usually be accepted upon his own word, or upon a critical examination of his doctrines or pretensions. There are numerous examples in history of illumined individuals who, as members of no organization; have contributed greatly to human good. The name of Socrates stands out, also Jacob Boehme, and Emanuel Swedenborg. In fact, many great systems of philosophy were founded by itinerant teachers who developed no organization or institution during their own lives.

As contrasted to this type are the numerous tribes of metaphysical "carpet-baggers" who are indeed parasites which have attached themselves to the tree of philosophy. To the average person who lacks the ability to distinguish with certainty the merit of various claims and pretensions, there is only one reasonable, safe course to bear in mind. The fraudulent metaphysician is usually finally convicted by his own words and actions. Ten years is about as long as any of them can function, and many of the most startling claimants do not last six months. That which does not stand the test of time is not worthy of acceptance. The metaphysical charlatan is generally not very ingenious and instinctively he follows lines of least resistance. Therefore, his misrepresentations fall into a few categories easily detected if subjected to critical thought. His claims may be considered as follows:

a: He is generally the only possessor of some very superlative truth which he has received direct from the Mahatmas of India or some equally august source difficult to check on.

b: He is willing to communicate this extraordinary knowledge to anyone, who has from five to twenty-five dollars, in ten easy lessons which lead inevitably to adeptship. He may have stocks and bonds, oil wells or laxatives as a side-line.

c: He nearly always infers that possession of the peculiar knowledge of which he is the sole owner (copyright applied for) will inevitably cause the individual fortunate enough to receive his instruction to become healthy, successful, wealthy and wise. From the time when he finishes the course, the student is predestined to opulence and a dominating will.

d: The means by which these miracles are accomplished include fancy breathing, assorted types of affirmations, "radiant thinking," the stimulation of the subconscious mind, raising the Kundalini, opening the third eye, and "going into the silence."

e: Numerous mechanical contrivances to aid in spirituality are sometimes offered for sale at reasonable prices, including psychic earmuffs to keep out the distractions of the outside world, phonograph records to impress the subconscious mind while asleep, etc. etc.

f: The newest, most refined form of metaphysical exploitation involves special revelations for the salvation of society from the impending social collapse. There is an unusual increase in the number of purported messages from various adepts at the present time—a state of affairs which must be viewed with some suspicion.

There are many variations in the technique of the pseudo-adepts, but always remember that any person at any time promising to any student or truth seeker any measure whatsoever of spiritual illumination is, of course, fraudulent or self-deluded. All spiritual development comes from within the individual, arising from discipline and self-improvement. No man can increase the spirituality of another. To attempt to do so is to disregard one of the most fundamental laws of nature—the law of Karma. Man earns wisdom by right thought and right action. The legitimate schools of the ancient wisdom, and the legitimate teachers of the doctrine offer spirituality to no one. They merely indicate a path of action, which, if followed with consecration and intelligence over a long period of years, will result in certain improvement of character and knowledge.

Esoteric secrets are never divulged by the ancient Mysteries or any of their emissaries to any student without a period of from five to ten years of probation. The prevalent idea that within a few months some individual, utterly without grounding in philosophy or comparative religion, can become worthy of personally contacting the Masters of Wisdom and receive instruction from them, leads to very sorry disillusionment.

To conclude, therefore, the problem of schools or individual teachers as sources of spiritual enlightenment, we can only warn truth seekers that they are confronted with a problem requiring an almost superhuman faculty of discrimination. The simpler frauds, of course, deceive only the utterly uninformed, but there are elaborate falsifications which have deceived persons of high integrity and a considerable measure of judgement. To keep the law of Karma constantly in mind, and avoid everything which even in small measure violates this universal law of compensation, will prove most protective. If you know within yourself that you are not ready for illumination and that you have not for many years practiced the disciplines of right thinking and right living, do not allow any man or organization to convince you that they can bestow upon you what you have not developed within yourself.

We will now pass to the second main division of our problem of gaining knowledge through external contact.

The LITERATURE OF THE AGES is, to the beginner in mystical studies, by far the safest approach. It is less dramatic than personal contact and less romantic than pseudo-adepts, but the hazards of deceit and misinformation are greatly reduced. The whole matter becomes susceptible of an impersonal analysis. We do not mean to suggest that all books are good or that all occult books are true. There are millions of comparatively worthless books, products of immature judgment, prejudice and unbalanced thought. On the other hand, there are certain great literary remains of the highest significance and of the greatest integrity.

The average man or woman can sit quietly in the relaxation of his own home or study and through the pages of a great book receive instruction from the very sources of this world's knowledge. The average person who pays twenty-five dollars to some charlatan or only partly informed teacher can secure better and more knowledge in his subject by spending a few evenings reading authentic textbooks from his free public library. If we are to study science, let us study it from its greatest masters—Bacon, Descartes, Copernicus, Vesalius, Huxley, etc. If we are to study philosophy and religion, let us derive it from its sources and prefer Buddha, Confucius, Lao Tze, Pythagoras or Plato to the petty sophistry of their uninformed modern exponents. Every student of the ancient wisdom should accumulate for himself a small but choice library of original source material. In our own wanderings, we have contacted hundreds of occult students who have spent comparatively large sums in the quest of spiritual knowledge. Only recently one person told me that she had just paid a hundred and fifty dollars to a fraudulent teacher in return for spiritual instruction which she never got. All she really received for her money was a serious nervous ailment brought about by trick breathing. This hundred and fifty dollars, if expended upon a few choice books, would have greatly enriched the person in the knowledge she so earnestly desired. She would have had to spend four years at least reading these books, studying them and thinking about them. She would have finished this task several times better informed than the itinerant teacher who cheated her out of the money.

People sometimes say that they do not want to study at home, that they find no pleasure in long evenings with heavy books. If such is the case, three or four kindred minds can study together, using the book as their text and teacher, and creating what the Greeks called a symposium. Larger groups are usually unfortunate even if sincere, but a half a dozen or less, meeting regularly over a long period, can accomplish a great deal. At least they avoid the exploitation and disillusionment met with when accepting the words of unknown and unqualified persons.

My experience with books in the field of occultism is reasonably wide. I have often thought about practical libraries for occult students, ranged according to levels of cost to meet the needs and financial limitations of students. An amazingly good library can be accumulated for as low as fifty dollars, and for five hundred dollars as a maximum a working laboratory of knowledge can be accumulated which will enlighten and enrich the thinking man or woman throughout life. Of course, if books are used as ornaments for the library shelf, they will do no good, but if studied intelligently and diligently and their principles applied, they will not only enrich the mind but will to great measure release the STREAMS OF INWARD INSPIRATION.

As a working basis, let us assume a library of ten books, carefully selected and fitted to the needs of the individual who is reasonably familiar with the general principles of philosophy and the occult sciences, but who desires to perfect and direct his knowledge:

1. *The History of Philosophy, by Thomas Stanley.

2. *Proclus on the Theology of Plato, translated by Thomas Taylor.

3. *The Restitution of Platonic Theology, by Thomas Taylor.

4. *Anacalypsis, by Godfrey Higgins.

5. Isis Unveiled, by H. P. Blavatsky

6. The Secret Doctrine, by H. P. Blavatsky.

7. Mankind, its Origin and Destiny, by an Anonymous Master of Arts of Oxford.

8. The Rosicrucian Cosmo-Conception, by Max Heindel.

9. Morals and Dogma of the Scottish Rite, by Albert Pike.

10. The Bhagavad-Gita, a fragment from the Hindu classic The Mahabharata.

At the present price of books, this library would cost about a hundred and seventy-five dollars. The four books marked with an asterisk (*) are expensive and can only be secured through a rare book dealer.

Any person possessing these ten volumes has a life work ahead of them to master and apply the knowledge contained in them. In the presence of such literature as this, words of power that will live through the ages, no student of the ancient wisdom needs to feel that he is without a means of knowing truth. The knowledge is here and awaits the industry of the student. No further revelation is necessary while these textbooks remain easily available and comparatively unread and undigested.

A good book is the modern occult student's safest approach to the teachings of those old masters whose wisdom we so sadly need in this world of materialism.

In our next letter, we shall take up the third branch of our study of external means of contacting wisdom. We shall consider Nature as a textbook of the divine law.

Yours very sincerely,

Manly P. Hall

LOS ANGELES, CALF. JUNE 1, 1935

Dear Friend,

In this letter, we shall continue the discussion of the theme of last month's article, namely. "Contacting sources of spiritual instruction." This month we are to consider Nature as the textbook of the divine law.

Those among the initiated pagans who venerated Nature as the visible manifestation of the eternally existing Universal Principle, were termed Pantheists —worshippers of Pan or Nature. In the Middle Ages Pantheism continued in the philosophies of the Alchemists, the Hermetists, and the Illuminati, members of these groups referring to themselves as Pan-Sophists or philosophers wise in the mysteries of Universal Nature.

It must not be supposed that the hierophants of Greek and Egyptian metaphysics taught their disciples a blind veneration for natural force, or sought to incline the minds of novices merely to the worship of external forms. Pantheism is not the worship of material nature but rather an effort to discover the true nature of divinity through an examination of those material consequences which are constantly flowing from the inscrutable center of the Universal One.

In his vision of the divine magnificence, Mohammed describes the innumerable veils which conceal the features of eternal Truth. As it is impossible for any man to behold God face to face, even the wisest must be content to gaze upon the innumerable veilings which obscure the splendid countenance of Being.

The pagans regarded divinity as the Great Architect. The material universe itself is described by the pagan philosophers as one of the noblest worlds of Divine Intellect. By coming to understand, to respect, even to adore Nature, the wisest of the ancients declared that they perceived more completely that splendid Reason which conceived the world and that vast Wisdom which maintains all things.

Paracelsus of Hohenheim, one of the last of the medieval philosophers, and one of the first thinkers of the modern world, called Nature the great textbook of Divine Mysteries. For the greater part of his short but eventful life Paracelsus wandered the by-ways of Europe gathering knowledge from the great storehouse of primitive fact. One of his mottoes was: "He who would study the book of Nature must walk its pages his feet." Nature is the unalterable factor in what many people feel to be a man-made world. Nature is inevitable. Nature is the divine criterion of all merit and demerit. By the mysterious processes of Nature, we come into being; by equally mysterious processes, we are preserved and perpetuated for a certain time; and in the end, by these same mysterious processes, we depart from this theatre of physical action. In our every thought and act, we are utterly dependent upon natural munificence. Men are constantly building up and tearing down the various institutions which together constitute the pageantry of empire; but all men, great and small, all enterprises, vast and humble, all processes, noble and ignoble, are circumscribed by a vast natural design from the boundaries of which they can never for an instant escape.

When men study the words of men, they gain a certain knowledge of passing things. Books are filled with opinions, and very often these opinions are limited in their usefulness to certain generations and decades. Nature, however, propounds inevitables. The book of Nature sets forth unchanging principles before which all human ingenuity must bow. Men can resist Nature for a little time, but in the end natural law is ever victorious.

To the philosopher, Nature is the instrument of a benevolent conspiracy. All the innumerable factors which together constitute the diffusion of Nature are active agencies of the Divine Purpose. The Divine Law and the Divine Mind supporting Nature are the agencies of an all-sufficient purpose. It is not given to man to fully understand this purpose, but to some men the magnitude of the Plan is at least dimly perceptible. Such men we term wise, for wisdom really is the perception of the plan of Being. He who understands the Plan becomes, to some measure, aware of the Planner. As the Hermetists said, "We perceive the Workman through the Works."

Students of mystical philosophy will never be without a sufficient inspiration while the panorama of Nature unfolds about them. False doctrines will come and go and many will be deceived thereby. There will be false gods and false prophets capturing the minds of the uninformed. There will be false gospels and false books, to lead astray the credulous. These morbid times are full of falacies. Yet, in the midst of all this confusion, no sincere and earnest disciple of the old doctrines need feel that the quest for truth is hopeless. The Ancient Wisdom, though so often perverted and obscured, remains evident and attainable so long as Nature endures. The Secret Doctrine is written in the sky, the most profound mysteries of Universal Law are revealed in the structure of leaf, flower and seed. A man cast away upon a desert island could restore the Secret Doctrine from a grain of sand did he possess the keys to accomplish this seeming miracle.

The Egyptians worshipped Nature in the form of the goddess Isis. They represented her as concealed by numerous veils, her body adorned with curious hieroglyphs. To the Greeks she was Kore or Ceres, the mother of the Eleusinian Mysteries. She was the mysterious Diana of the Ephesians. To Christendom she is Mary, the Virgin Mother of the Messianic Incarnation. Always she is the source of that moral nutriment by which the wellbeing of the human soul is assured.

It is natural for man to overlook the obvious. Men have made so many legislations in the last few thousand years that they seem to have forgotten the inevitability of natural law. Civilization, verging towards empire, has ignored the laws governing, that very earth from which civilization has reared itself. Man, the child, has forgotten Nature, the parent. He has built a tower of Babel, where he should have erected a temple to the Universal Mystery. By this building, he has achieved only to a confusion of tongues when he should have attained to a universal concord.

On a certain occasion, Socrates was walking with some disciples along a busy thoroughfare in Athens. The old stoical philosopher was beginning a discourse and one of his disciples, fearing that the confusion of the street would distract his master, said to him, "Before you begin this teaching let us seek a place suitable for instruction." Instantly Socrates replied, "The place where thou art is always suitable for instruction." This incident has great significance for the modern truth-seeker. In ancient Athens various teachers had groves and squares and other retreats in and about the city. Plato preferred the Lyceum, Aristotle the race-track at the Gymnasium. Plato always taught while sitting, Aristotle, while walking, and Diogenes talked only while in his tub. Socrates aimed his remarks against the opinion that various places had special virtue, that men were nearer to God or Truth in one place than another, and that divine concerns could only be spoken of in shrines or temples. To Socrates, philosophy was so essentially an inner mystery of consciousness that he is famed for the declaration: "Wherever a man desires to know, that is the place proper for his education; whenever he desires to know, that is the time proper for his instruction."

In the modern world, the study of the various departments of Nature has become the proper field of science. A number of "exact" sciences have been established and developed whereby phenomena are classified and the various forces at work throughout Nature cataloged and examined. Science has accumulated a vast body of formal knowledge and anyone desirous of understanding the complicated workings of the material universe can realize his desire by applying himself to one or more of the sciences. Astronomy will reveal to him the mechanics of the heavens; geology, the formation of the earth; anthropology, the origin and development of the human race. No philosopher will deny the significance of the body of knowledge amassed by science.

Philosophy differs from science, however, chiefly in the matter of the conclusions arising from this accumulated mass of physical knowledge. Science READS THE BOOK OF NATURE BUT DOES NOT UNDERSTAND what it reads. All too often, therefore, profundity of scientific learning inclines to atheism or, at least, to a morbid agnosticism. The mechanistic theory in science, which views the whole universal process as a sort of perpetual motion device, is an utterly insufficient explanation of existence and its laws. If scientists could only realize that the knowledge which they have accumulated is not complete in itself but depends upon the metaphysical philosophies of the ancients for its interpretation, they would be rescued from the numerous uncertainties which now beset them.

The mystery of divinity comprehends three other mysteries as aspects of itself. God, as Nature, is visibly manifested through a diversity of phenomena. God, as Thought, is infinitely diffused as the reason in all things. God, as Spirit, is the hidden power which sustains all things, as intrinsic life. We perceive God without as Nature, God within as Self, and the very faculty with which we perceive is itself divine and acts as a mediator between its own extremes. Philosophy is not itself a body of knowledge but rather an interpreter of knowledge. Knowledge does not actually become fact, philosophically speaking, until its relationship with the divine. Whole has been demonstrated. That, which is perceived by the senses, is Nature. Nature contemplated by the mind reveals its processes and procedures. These in turn, comprehended by the inner Self, become wisdom.

No true and enlightened system of philosophy will ever depart from the laws of Nature. The ancient philosophers described the vast body of Nature as supported upon an intricate structure of law. In Thibet, the Lamas say that the material creation is upheld upon a foundation of crossed thunderbolts. These thunderbolts symbolize the dynamic agencies of the cosmic process. By the Egyptians, the planets were regarded as divine Beings, focal points of cosmic energy and universal law. Following their astro-philosophical theory, we can associate planets and laws according to the following arrangement:

1. Neptune: Periodicity. Existence is divided into cycles and sub-cycles measured by the recurrences of certain celestial phenomena. Neptune as the slowest moving of the planets, requiring the greatest time to complete his revolution, became emblematic of the standard of all cyclic and periodic return. As the ancients expressed it, "All things have beginnings, midmost states, and ends." Also, all ends are beginnings and all beginnings are ends. In India, the cosmic cycles of time, in which worlds, continents, races and empires rise and fall, are termed KALPAS and YUGAS. By the Greeks, they are termed Ages. The whole creative process is supported upon a framework of inconceivable time and duration factors.

2. Uranus: Alternation. Throughout the entire universal procedure, the law of alternation is constantly at work. All natures pass from one extreme to another and in the course of this pendulum-like swing, go through a numerous complexity of experiences. By alternation of the earth's poles, all parts of the planet's surface are going through constant climatic modification. Through alternation of sex in reincarnation, the human soul swings gradually from one cycle of experience to another. Every condition which arises in society breeds its opposite. Every intemperance inclines towards an opposite intemperance. Existence is a vast, ever-swinging pendulum moving backward and forward with the ebb and flow of the cosmic tide.

3. Saturn: Cause and Effect. In the Mysteries, Chronos or Saturn was regarded as the crudest and most unforgiving of divinities, devourer of his own children. He represents the immutability of the cosmic plan and in no way is this immutability more evident than in the law of cause and effect, from which there can be no deviation of any bind— a law without exception, compromise or modification. "As ye sow, so shall ye reap," says the Christian Scriptures. "Effect follows cause as the wheel of the cart follows the foot of the oxen" says the Buddhist Canons. Yet this law, though apparently so severe, is in reality the most kindly and just of edicts, for it insures that in good, as well as in evil, that which a man earns shall inevitably come to him.

4. Jupiter: Evolution. The law of evolution may be defined as the expanding of natures from within themselves, outwardly, Jupiter was the god of growth and expansion. Evolution is unfoldment. It is the externalizing of internal divinity. It is God growing up in forms and causing these forms to increase their own dimensions that they may be adequate for the truth growing up within them. Every form in nature is evolving and by evolution is returning again to its own source—the infinite perfection within which

it was originally individualized. Evolution is the process of becoming ever more sufficient to the need of that energy resident within the evolving form.

5. Mars: Karma. The law of Karma is in some respects to be differentiated from Cause and Effect. Cause and Effect as governed by Saturn is entirely impersonal, that is, it transcends the moral value. Karma, or the law of compensation, is Cause and Effect applied directly to man or to a self-motivating moral agent. Karma comes into manifestation with the development of the conscious mind. Nature never chooses to do evil because it is ruled completely by law. Man, possessing the power to choose to do that which is wrong, creates thereby Karma, which takes the form of Cause and Effect as a medium of punishment or retribution. Thus, Mars becomes the devil, punishing misdeeds. Saturn's law of Cause and Effect infers no element of punishment, merely inevitable ebb and flow.

6. Sun: Reincarnation. The annual birth, death and resurrection of the Sun causes it to be the proper symbol of the luminous Ego of man which moves from body to body in the mystery of Reincarnation. Rebirth is the law of evolution applied to the Self within man, which, surviving disintegration of the physical form, builds nobler mansions and lives on through the ages in new bodies suitable to its needs.

7. Venus: Harmony and Rhythm. Nature, in the achievement of her inevitable ends, moves gloriously and directly, never for a moment deviating from the certainty of her course. Causes flow into effects with a majesty and beauty, and all of Nature's processes have about them a grace and harmonious rhythm. The ancients, therefore, declared that Nature's way being the absolute standard of beauty, all creatures should cultivate harmony and rhythm as attributes of the divine nature.

8. Mercury: Equilibrium. In the old books of the Cabbalists, it is written that all unbalanced forces perish in the Void. Unbalance leads to destruction. Equilibrium or poise conserves resource and achieves permanence. Mercury as mind is the reconciler of opposites. He who achieves balance achieves power. Equilibrium is an immovable foundation upon which to build an enduring structure of thought and action. All extremes must be overcome. Equilibrium is immortality.

9. The Moon: Generation. All egos entering into the physical universe must obey the law of generation. All material forms are created according to the patterns and principles peculiar to what Plato termed the generating sphere. At this stage of evolution, the law of generation infers that all bodies

must be built according to one law or pattern. This is the celebrated Forty-seventh Proposition of Euclid. Man himself, termed in China the child of heaven and earth, is the progeny of the first pair of opposites—spirit and matter.

10. The Earth: In the old philosophies the earth had no law peculiar to it but was the laboratory in which the nine laws manifest themselves in infinite combinations. The material universe is really the embodiment of law. The laws of Nature are the impulses resident in the Divine Intellect manifesting as the movers of atoms and builders of worlds. When the student grasps the mystical significance of these laws, he has established his philosophy upon a permanent and sufficient foundation.

Yours very sincerely,

Manly P. Hall

QUESTIONS AND ANSWERS

QUESTION—Is theology the same as religion?

ANSWER—We like to distinguish distinctly between the term theology and the term religion. By theology we like to understand any organized system of dogma, creed, ceremonial, ritual and sacrament constituting an ecclesiasticism. By religion, we like to understand man's inner urge to venerate the beautiful, serve the good and see God in everything. When a religion is crystallized and organized into a sect and divides itself from the beliefs of other men, it becomes a theology. The great World Teachers brought philosophical and religious revelation which gradually became instituted and established as theological systems. Man is naturally a religious animal, but he is a theological animal only by heredity and environment. There is only one religion in the world but there are many theologies which have risen up as competitive organizations, each claiming to be holier than the other. Take, for example, Christianity. The Christian religion consists of two commandments: to love God and to love one another. The simple living of these two commandments constitutes Christianity as a religion. In the last nineteen hundred years hundreds of sects have risen, many of them greatly complicated and having elaborate systems and statutes of observances. Today we have over two hundred sects in Christendom, all more or less competitive and greatly divided. These are theologies. To the degree that a spiritual revelation is complicated and divided, to that degree is becomes theological. To the degree that it remains simple and united, to that degree it remains religious.

QUESTION—We have a three-year-old daughter. What religious training do you recommend?

ANSWER—Small children, too young to understand any of the philosophical truths of life, are best taught by a beautiful example of enlightened living in the home as the child becomes a little older, she can be taught that religion means, first of all, living beautifully and nobly, and that a beautiful life is the most acceptable offering to the God of truth and beauty dwelling in all parts of the universe. Under existing conditions, we would recommend that the spiritual education of the child remain as a sacred duty of the parent for there are no organizations at the present time that can compare with enlightened parental influence. As the child grows older, she should also be taught that religion is an inner relationship between the person herself and the spirit that dwells in her own heart. No special sectarian religious training should be given to the child. If in later years, the child, grown up to mature judgment, chooses to affiliate with some religious movement, that choice should result from mature judgment and not from parental influence. It is a tragedy to set a child's mind in any theological rut before the child has sufficient individuality to resist this influence and choose its own course of action.

QUESTION—Is it possible to reconcile the idea of a personal God with the impersonal God?

ANSWER—The answer to this question is largely a matter of viewpoint. Creation is God personalized. God is creation impersonalized. If you mean by a personal God an old man with whiskers seated on a golden throne, then such a concept is irreconcilable with philosophy because to philosophers such a concept of deity is purely idolatrous. An idol can exist in the mind just as surely as it can in wood or stone. Idolatry is the personalization of universal principles. The impersonal God of the wise is that Sovereign Good, inconceivable and immeasurable, which abides in everything, enlivens and supports all things, ensouls existence, and, in the terms of Brahmin metaphysics, extends to the very circumference of space. Justice is impersonal, truth is impersonal, law is impersonal, virtue is impersonal. All the great and noble instances which lift man to the heights of universal achievement are impersonal. Universal survival depends upon the impersonality of that vast Cause which supports the entire scheme of life. Yet the impersonal God is not distant; in fact, is far more intimate than a personal divinity could possibly be. The God of philosophy is not anywhere, but everywhere. At a certain stage of human growth, man achieves to the realization of the insufficiency and inconsistency of a personal God. The mind then demands an impersonal agent at the foundation of action. It is not the purpose of philosophy to reconcile the concept of a personal and an impersonal God; only growth, development, and unfoldment within the individual can result in that state of mind in which the personal divinity fades away, and consciousness discovers that vast and all-sufficient Spirit which abides in the star and the grain of sand.

QUESTION—Can science be reconciled with religion?

ANSWER—Science and religion were identical in origin, are divided in their present state, and will be united again to become identical in their ultimate. Religion is concerned with the moral values of existence; science with the physical values of existence. Every physical value is the outcome of a moral impulse. The Divine Spirit of religion created the material world of science. In the last analysis, there is no clear line of demarcation where God leaves off and Nature begins. Divinity in itself is Spirit; divinity in form is Nature. Religion has become crystallized into theological institutions which maintain themselves to a great degree by magnifying points of difference. Science has been crystallized into institutions which have isolated themselves from the arts and ethics of the race and have dedicated their time and effort to exploration and classification of material phenomena. It will probably become a time before the church and the laboratory will recognize that they are essentially identical. Therefore, the only way that we can reconcile science and religion at the present time is in the nature of an enlightened man. A person who has accomplished this reconciliation within himself is properly called a philosopher because he has recognized that the purpose of all knowledge is to discover God, and that from this discovery must arise, finally, systems of thought dedicated to the perfection of man through accumulated All opposites of learning are reconciled in the soul of the wise man.

QUESTION—Can past Karma be escaped by present good deeds?

ANSWER—According to the Ancient Wisdom that which is done cannot be undone. No philosophical system worthy of the name would fall into the fallacy of vicarious atonement. Nature's bookkeeping system has in it no place for erasures. The motive behind present good deeds should never be to escape past Karma, but rather to prevent the making of more bad Karma. An individual whose present life is filled with efforts to improve character and increase the measure of meritorious action is establishing a solid philosophical foundation of well-being to be enjoyed in future existences. This explains a mystery which confuses many students. A person will say. "All my life I have done good to others and all my life I have suffered misfortune; where is the honesty and integrity of nature?" We bring forward from past existences Karma which must be lived out. As we have injured, so we must suffer. Today we are building Karma for tomorrow, and if our present life is dedicated to enlightened thinking and living, we are more apt to enjoy the results thereof in a future existence than in this one. However, very often the good deeds of this life have their reward even here. Not only do we bring forward from the past evil Karma but good Karma; consequently, the average life is a complex of fortune and misfortune, due to the inconsistencies and ignorance of previous lives.

QUESTION—What is the purpose of baptism?

ANSWER—The sacrament of baptism descended to Christendom from the old pagan Mysteries where it was originally a symbol of purification through water or the cleansing of the body prior to the entrance into a holy place. In the Tabernacle Mysteries of the Jews there was a great laver of purification in the courtyard wherein the priests bathed themselves before donning the vestments of sanctity. Even to this day the Mohammedan mosques have in their courtyard's large tanks of water like pools wherein the faithful must wash their feet before participating in the services. The Egyptians recognized two symbolical baptisms: the first of water, symbolizing the purification of the body through strict observance and physical regeneration; the second of fire, symbolizing the enlightenment of the spirit or the descent of consciousness. These baptisms are mentioned in the Gospels. Baptism is a purely symbolical sacrament, a constant reminder that only the pure and the clean are worthy to enter into the knowledge of God. The literal acceptance of baptism as a method of washing out original sin is purely theological. The original sin is ignorance which must be washed out, or the body purified therefrom, by the disciplines of wisdom. Truth purifies the life and fits the one who possesses it to enter into the inner sanctuary of the mystery temple. All of the sacraments are similarly symbolical, having no virtue apart from a course of action, which they imply. Baptism should always be regarded as the sacrament of self-purification by means of right thinking, right emotion, and right action.

QUESTION—Would you advise a man to leave civilization who cannot make spiritual progress among a corrupt and evil populace?

ANSWER—It is not possible for anyone to run away from life. There is an old Arabian fable of a man who sought to escape from the evils of existence only to discover that the shadow of them pursued him to the most distant parts of the earth. At last, he learned that this shadow was his own body and that the one evil that no man can escape is himself. Philosophy does not advise truth-seekers to run away from experience, but rather, to use wisdom to face experience more intelligently. These stirring and difficult times in which we live are important to the soul growth of each individual. Philosophy is not merely a studying of books or a thinking of beautiful thoughts. Philosophy is living well in a world which tests the capacity of the individual to live well. Life itself is an initiation into the sanctuary of the Divine Mystery. As neophytes of old were tested as to courage and integrity and wisdom by various trials devised by the priests, so modern truth-seekers are tested by the adversity of life. An individual who cannot achieve where he is cannot achieve anywhere else. Achievement is an inner strength rising up secure and sufficient. Strength comes from action and adversity. The years ahead will be trying years. The steel of the human soul is tempered by the flame of suffering.

QUESTION—How can a drone become useful at fifty? Now that I understand things better, I want to be useful.

ANSWER—The first thing for you to do is to forget that you are fifty. Remember that you are an eternal Self; that before the world existed you were, and that after the world ends, you will still be. Time is an illusion and greatness rises above time. Many of the greatest men and women of the world accomplished little, if anything, before fifty. When you think of accomplishment in philosophical terms you are thinking of something that transcends time and place and becomes part of a cosmic plan of action, extending through hundreds of lives. Take stock of yourself. What have you learned in the fifty years of the present life? What do you know that others ought to know? What can you do that needs to be done? Remember that in the great craft of the Temple Builders, we all begin as apprentices. Our first task must always be something small and comparatively insignificant. The beginning of wisdom is to do the thing at hand. You may still need to spend time in the perfection of your own disposition, the mastery of temperament and attitude. You may still have responsibilities to others around you which have not been fulfilled. The example of what you have accomplished and what philosophy has done for you may be a great inspiration to those with whom you come in contact. Thinly noble thoughts, dream beautiful dreams, labor constructively from day to day, and when you are ready for a greater accomplishment, the work that you are to do will come to hand. The universe always has work for those who are qualified to perform it.

QUESTION—Is it possible to separate spirituality and wisdom? In other words, can a person be spiritually perfect and yet not possess all knowledge?

ANSWER—It is not possible to separate spirituality and wisdom any more than it is possible to prevent a cause from producing its effect. Spirituality actually means that the individual lives or exists upon the level of his spiritual nature or is possessed by the divinity within him. Divinity can have no ignorance within it. God cannot lack anything. Therefore, wisdom is an inevitable correlative of complete spiritual development. The difficulty which has arisen and causes this question lies in the misunderstanding of the nature of spirituality. We are assured in the Scriptures that there is "not one perfect." We know that, at this stage of evolution, it is impossible for a human being to be absolutely perfect either spiritually or physically, for perfection itself is an ultimate, far from our finite state. A person may possess a certain measure of spirituality, but even in the wisest, this measure is hopelessly incomplete. To the degree that we have spiritual development, to the same degree, we must have an extension of knowledge. There are certain metaphysical groups which promise "cosmic consciousness" as the result of metaphysical exercises. We have met many people claiming to possess this "cosmic consciousness," but a brief conversation with them clearly indicates that they are suffering only from mild hallucination. Cosmic consciousness is all-knowing, and no secret of Nature can be concealed from those who possess even a moderate degree of true illumination. Any person, claiming to possess cosmic consciousness and at the same time manifesting all the limitations and imperfections of the flesh, must be suspected of imposture or delusion.

QUESTION—Do people appreciate only what they pay well for? Please explain the money principle in connection with spiritual instruction.

ANSWER—All neophytes entering the ancient Mystery Temples brought with them valuable gifts or such as they had. Not because the gifts themselves were regarded as payment for instruction, but because only the individual who was willing to sacrifice the best that he had for that which he desired to know was worthy of instruction. Money is a symbol of value in this modern world. The average person prizes it above every other possession. Therefore, it is proper and suitable that he should give it as a symbol of sacrifice and appreciation for the priceless treasure which he receives. Any person having much and selfishly refusing to support adequately that which he believes, need not hope for any great measure of illumination. It is not the lack of the gift that will stand in his way, but the lack of the spirit of giving.

LOS ANGELES, JULY 1, 1935

QUESTION—What advice do you give to a person who desires to apply himself to a serious study of the Ancient Wisdom Teachings?

ANSWER—The desire for wisdom is in itself the most commendable of human emotions, but in too many cases, this desire comes to naught through ignorance and misunderstanding. We must not only earnestly and unselfishly desire truth but we must create within our own natures an ethical environment suitable for the reception of spiritual knowledge. If a building is to stand, it must be raised upon an adequate foundation, and if human character is to withstand the shocks of circumstance, it must also be built upon a firm and true foundation. No man can know more than he himself is. That with which we understand is the measure of our understanding. Before it is possible for an individual to perceive clearly the mysteries of the inner life, he must develop the faculties for this perception. From the most ancient times, the priests of the Mystery Temples were the custodians of the disciplines of philosophy. These disciplines were revealed only to disciples who had proved themselves worthy of such instruction. There is much more to the study of philosophy than merely listening, reading, and accepting. The first step in the study of the Ancient Wisdom Teachings is not the quest of knowledge but the preparation of self to receive knowledge. This is where most truth seekers make their first mistake. With their eyes turned towards the heavens, they rush ecstatically towards "illumination," only to stumble, like Thales, into the ditch of their own unpreparedness. We know thousands of people who want to be wise but very few of these people seem capable of understanding that before wisdom must come the capacity for wisdom. Illumination is only possible in an organism that has fitted itself for illumination; nor does one so fit himself by hoping, wishing or listening. As an athlete must train himself in order to excel in bodily prowess, so the student of philosophy must put his thoughts, emotions and actions under specialized discipline if he is to develop philosophical strength. Between the modern truth seeker and the goal to which he aspires are numerous pitfalls and dilemmas. False prophets lead astray the unwary, conflicting doctrines perplex the uninformed, and a host of doubts and uncertainties weaken the resolution. Hundreds of students afflicted with these numerous problems have asked me to straighten out for them the tangled course of learning. The usual complaint of the confused goes somewhat like this—"How am I going to know if this teacher is telling the truth? How can I determine what sect to foin? How can I be sure that this book is reliable? Among a thousand claims, pretensions, boasts and persuasions, how am I to perceive clearly the straight and certain way that leads to light?"

It is very difficult to reason with people suffering from religious glamour. For example, you may spend hours explaining to such a person that a certain swami's breathing exercises will lead to nervous derangements and mental unbalance rather than illumination, only to find him a few weeks later studying the same exercises from another swami. It is impossible to save anyone from his own foolishness. If by some miracle you can pick him out of a present evil, he only falls into the next snare that is encountered. Most modern metaphysicians suffer from an incurable attack of falling sickness. They waste their time and their means on pseudoprophets and false gods. They prefer insipid platitudes to hard work.

Now at first thought it may seem that the real cause of trouble is the false prophet, but upon more mature reflection it is evident that false prophets can only thrive upon the stupidity and gullibility of thoughtless mortals, weak in the faculty of common sense. This leads to the major conclusion:

A person incapable of discriminating between a true and false doctrine is unfitted for any form of esoteric instruction.

This sweeping statement may offend a class of people who feel that their souls are much more highly evolved than their intelligence, but the truth remains that a man incapable of unmasking a fake mahatma is scarcely in a position to unveil the mysteries of the Cosmos. If a student were to ask how to protect himself against the insidious effect of corrupt doctrines, I should say—If you are thoroughly, devotedly and unswervingly dedicated to the acceptance of the immutability of the law of karma you are above the contaminating influence of ninety-nine percent of fraudulent metaphysicians. If you believe in Karma, you know that you can never avoid the results of action or enjoy unmerited advantages. The universe, gods and men bow before the inevitable edict of Karma. There are no vicarious atonements or exceptions in creation. Law is final, absolute and immutable. The disciple who takes his stand upon this fact will never wander far from the truth, but he who departs even for an instant from this certainty plunges into a sea of troubles.

The doctrine of Karma is sufficiently simple and familiar that even the average layman is capable of appreciating its integrity. Nearly all students of metaphysics pretend to accept the statement of Karma as we find it in the Bible: "As ye sow, so shall ye reap." Yet in practice, there are literally hundreds of metaphysical movements which seek in one way or another to undermine the teaching of this law by doctrines of "special dispensation." To compromise truth is to deny God, and philosophy has no place in it for any cult which seeks to compromise with the law of Cause and Effect.

A pertinent example of what we mean by compromising the teaching of the law of Karma will illustrate this general thought. A metaphysical teacher claiming to speak the name of a great adept recently stated that the long periods of probation and preparation prior to esoteric instruction, demanded in the old Mystery Schools, were no longer necessary for students of the spiritual sciences. By a new dispensation, this adept would open the doors of the inner mysteries at the present time to all earnest souls. (! ! !)

Thousands of sincere people, forgetful of the law of Karma, have been intrigued by this program. Their faculties of discrimination are numbed by the name of the illustrious adept used to further the ideas of this "teacher." An informed student can only have one attitude on this matter. No adept of the Great White Lodge could possibly promulgate a doctrine inconsistent with the law of Karma; and no man, adept, or even God, can in any way modify the working of that law. Adepts do not make the laws of nature—they serve them. The probationary rules and rites of the old Mysteries are as much an inevitable part of man's spiritual education as infancy and childhood are a part of his physical development. As well say that a human being can reach maturity without childhood and adolescence as that a human being can reach initiation without probationship and discipleship. If I were personally convinced (which I certainly am not) that the adept referred to had actually made the statements attributed to him, I would still not believe them. Rather l would derive the authority for my attitude from the words of Gautama Buddha who stated on one occasion: "I will not accept a doctrine because the learned have so stated it, nor will I accept it because the gods themselves have so spoken; I will accept it only because it is true."

Euclid the Megarian was once asked by Ptolemy, King of Egypt, if there was a short way to master geometry. The philosopher instantly replied, "Sire, there is no royal road to knowledge."

The words of Euclid apply perfectly to the mysteries of philosophy. There is no royal road to truth. There is no shortcut to God. There is no patent formula for the achievement of wisdom. All things grow and unfold. Truth and wisdom in man must likewise develop according to the laws of their own natures. True students of the great doctrines which bring about the emancipation of the human soul are not interested in "royal roads." A man seeking wisdom seeks the most valuable thing in the world. He desires a treasure not easily to be gained but in value above all other treasures of the earth. He knows that those who "live the life shall know the doctrine." Dedicated to self-improvement and the establishment of his own life upon the immutable foundations of integrity he is unmoved and uninfluenced by vain promises and empty words.

It must always be remembered that while philosophy has in it many superphysical doctrines, it has never included any supernatural speculations. There are no miracles in nature. There are effects the causes of which are unknown to us, yet each of these effects is the outworking of a law in itself consistent with the effect which it produces. Any person who waits for a miracle to bring about his perfection, or expects to perfect himself by miraculous means, will be sadly disillusioned in the course of time. The admonition of the old sages still holds true and will continue to do so until the end of time: "Each man must work out his own salvation with diligence."

Many novices in the study of occult science come to the conclusion that they are making small advancement unless they practice "development" exercises to stimulate some aspect of "cosmic consciousness" within themselves. There are also many foolish enough to think that visions, voices, and other psychic phenomena are indications of unfolding spiritual powers. Let no earnest seeker be deceived by such fantasies. The achievement of wisdom is man's coming of age and it is natural for that individual to be wise who has set up the causes of wisdom in himself. To one who has not set up these causes, wisdom is not only unnatural, but impossible.

The truth concerning spiritual exercises is that they are useless and even dangerous unless part of a carefully planned and intelligently directed program of self-improvement to stimulate, psychic centers in the body by breathing, concentration, meditation, etc., without first bringing the entire nature under the "rule of reason," is to endanger life and health. No man is greater than the sum of his own parts, and breathing by some mystic formula cannot make a man greater than he is.

Luther Burbank called man the "human plant." Like some flower of the field the human soul unfolds under the benefic influences of nature. Yet it is not alone the sun which nourishes the plant, nor the rain, nor the dark earth, nor the moon, nor the stars, nor the wind, but rather all of these together in proper measure and proportion. So, in the human plant, it is not alone the air man breathes that sustains him, nor the sidereal diffusion, nor his food, nor his thought, nor his emotion, nor his action, nor his aspiration, but rather all these together, in balanced combination. To make any real progress in this greatest of all sciences, the student of philosophy must improve in each and every one of his parts. It is not sufficient that he tries to stimulate a few nerve plexus and feel that in this manner he has become acceptable in the sight of the law.

When Plato established his Academy, he caused to be inscribed above the gate the words: "Let none ignorant of geometry enter here." Pythagoras would permit none to become a member of his community who had not achieved excellence in mathematics, astronomy and music in addition to the moral virtues. Each applicant for admission to the ancient Mystery Temples was expected to possess a high standard of character and ability. Celsus, in a passage preserved by Origen, declares that those who call man to the mysteries of the Eternal God proclaim as follows: "Let him approach whose hands are pure, and whose words are wise. And again, others proclaim: Let him approach who is pure from all wickedness, whose soul is not conscious of any evil, and who leads a just and upright life. And these things are proclaimed by those who promise a purification from error."

It is not my intention to seem pessimistic or to discourage sincere men and women seeking spiritual light, but it is only fair to the student himself that he should understand the requirements for admission into the ranks of the philosophic elect. The average metaphysician is hopelessly unqualified for the pursuit of knowledge. He is willing, hopeful, and as kindly as his disposition will permit, but in most cases, he is so lacking in the fundamentals of character and ability that he could not have been accepted into any of the schools of mystical philosophy about which he reads so avidly. I have heard many say, "If I had only lived in the days of Pythagoras! If I could only have known Plato! If I could only have sat at the feet of Buddha!" Yet if these same people had lived in those days and possessed only their present qualifications, they could not have been admitted into the schools of any of these masters.

Fortunately, the disease of ignorance is not incurable. Those who wish to be the disciples of the Ancient Teachings today can fit themselves for the philosophic life by following the same procedure which twenty-four hundred years ago prepared disciples for initiation into the Pythagorean rites.

Let us now consider those offerings which each neophyte must bring to the gates of the "Everlasting House." There are fourteen requisites—seven of the inner life which are termed character, and seven of the outer life which are termed acquirements. The seven inner requisites arise from self-discipline, and the seven outer requisites from the direction of ability to the mastery of the arts and sciences. A person who has achieved to a reasonable proficiency in the fourteen requisites may be described as capable of becoming aware of the esoteric keys to the secrets of life. Let those who do not possess the fourteen requisites first achieve to these before they demand admission to the House of Light. We shall first consider the seven requisites of character:

1. INTEGRITY. In philosophy, the term integrity signifies much more than the ordinary term honesty. Honesty may be an only acceptance of certain standards of right and wrong and obedience thereto, but integrity is honesty illumined by inward realization. Integrity is the irresistible inward impulse to do that which is wise, noble, and beautiful. It lifts the life above blind obedience to manmade law and establishes every thought and action upon the foundation of Abiding Justice. Integrity also infers perfect consistency between inward impulse and outward action. The outward life is dominated by inner conviction and there is no interval of difference between the beauty in the soul and the nobility in the outward deed. Integrity is the living of truth, or possibly for the novice the living of that which is the nearest to truth which he knows. A man who believes in fine, spiritual principles and then lives a code of action inconsistent with these principles lacks integrity though he may be honest in his weights and measures. All too many truth seekers claim noble standards and live petty and intolerant codes. Such a person might study mysticism for a hundred lives, yet, not having learned to live a gentle and noble life, his theorizing's and meditating's are in vain. The old sages became embodiments of the beliefs and traditions which they served. No one can really have beautiful thoughts in their souls without their lives being beautified thereby, for all outward living is molded over inward impulse. Integrity is the rationalizing of the inner life so that all which emerges from it is just, enlightened, and true.

2. DISCRIMINATION. Out of integrity arises discrimination, for that life

which is founded in truth is lived in harmony with truth. The virtue of discrimination lies in the power it bestows to determine the comparative dignity of values. The end of discrimination is to invariably discover right and choose it from among conflicting and confusing opinions. Discrimination to a certain degree, is judgment. To another degree, it is clear vision, and to a considerable measure, it is courage. Discrimination leads to conviction and bestows the courage of conviction. He who possesses discrimination can never be victimized by the illusionary values of this mortal sphere. All of the old philosophers declared discrimination to be invaluable to the pursuit of wisdom. A person incapable of discriminating between the various doctrines which have been promulgated in different centuries and civilizations can never hope to discover the truth. Philosophy is a service of truth and no man can serve well that which he cannot discover surely. Discrimination destroys false gods; it releases the soul from bondage to opinions; it emancipates man from a thousand errors. To use a poetic phrase, discrimination picks unerringly the polar star from a galaxy of constellations. In modern metaphysics, thousands of student's drift from cult to cult upon a tide of moods and emotions. We cannot truly progress until we chart the course of our purposes. Discrimination removes the uncertainties from action. We drift no longer, but, steering a sure course, come at last to the safe haven we have sought for.

3. APPLICATION is the capacity for intelligent persistence. It infers both continuity and continuousness. It also conveys the thought of one-pointedness and thoroughness of effort. In Western civilization, the tenor of life is subject to constant interruption. The average individual is torn between many purposes. He attempts to scatter his faculties and his vital resources over much too large an area of activity, and in his attempt to do everything, does nothing well. By developing the power of application, the mind is secured from the hazards of distraction and interruption. Without application, there can be no organized intensity of effort and without organized intensity, there can be no great accomplishment in philosophy. Application, however, does not mean that a student should think of nothing but his philosophy twenty-four hours a day, three hundred and sixty-five days a year, nor that his whole time should be devoted to study, reading or contemplation of abstract truths. A life unreasonably immersed in learning is apt to be fruitless and unbalanced. Learning, to be of the greatest value, must be tested by application. The philosopher not only devotes hours to the absorption of knowledge, he must also spend years in the application of

knowledge to its reasonable ends. A healthy, normal existence infers a fine balance between effort and relaxation. The word application is concerned not with the duration of effort primarily, but rather with the whole-soulness of effort. In music, for example, certain hours must be given to practice and failure to observe this routine is fatal to technique. On the other hand, it is perfectly possible for the musician to over-practice and through this excess destroy the individuality and soul quality of his performance. Application involves a fine discrimination, the skill to judge the routine necessary to build a solid foundation, and courage to interrupt this routine before it destroys the individual qualities of the mind. Remember that philosophy is an art as well as a science. While the processes of thinking are bounded by certain rules, these rules, if over-emphasized, result in a bondage to process, and soul power is easily destroyed when inner impulse is wholly sacrificed to prescribed method.

4. PATIENCE. Application naturally infers patience, and patience is indeed a power of the soul. Without patience, nothing that is real or worthwhile can be accomplished. Patience is resignation to the inevitable processes of law. It should not destroy enthusiasm, but should curb all extremes of emotion, bringing about a gentle acceptance of the facts of existence. Nearly all students of metaphysical subjects are lured away from reason by the impatience of mind and heart. The most fatal delusion of metaphysics is belief in short cuts to perfection. Many erroneous doctrines are catering to the impatience of the human soul. No individual who is willing to allow only one, or five, ten or fifty years for the perfecting of himself should ever take up the study of philosophy. The Ancient Wisdom Teachings measure the progress of the individual not in terms of years, but in terms of lives. It has taken thousands of millions of years to bring man up through the numerous stages of evolution to his present state, and it will require millions of years more to lift him to those divine heights to which his heart aspires. There is something pathetically ridiculous about people who are able to believe that they can attain "cosmic consciousness" in a few short lessons. I have met many sincere but benighted souls who, after studying a smattering of the occult sciences for a few years, are waiting breathlessly for initiation, which they believe is "right around the corner." As one expressed it, after a few months study, "I expect the veil between the visible and invisible worlds to drop at any moment." Patience is the test of character, courage and understanding. It is not the desire of the wise to build hastily, but rather to build well. "Psychic shysters" will go out of business when neophytes

in metaphysics understand the words of the Greek philosopher who said, "Make philosophy thy existence." The old sage did not say thy life work, or thy trade or thy profession, or thy effort for a certain number of years. He used the term "thy existence" to infer that the life of wisdom goes on from incarnation to incarnation, becoming a part of the very self, transcending all limitations of time and place. Students of the Ancient Wisdom will still be students a million years from now, for as all life is a process of achieving never consummated by ultimate achievement, so philosophy is a process of ever learning to which experience there is no conceivable end. The impatient novice tries a new system of "development" when "illumination" fails to arrive after a few months of study, but the soul, wise with patience, which has risen above these illusions, rejoices in the perception of some small improvement at the end of many years of patient living.

5. MODERATION. All of the great masters of wisdom have warned their disciples of the dangers of immoderate attitudes. To Buddha the philosophic life was the Middle Path between all intemperance's of impulse. To Aristotle, sufficient learning was the Golden Mean and equilibrium overcoming every aspect of excess. Socrates expressed the thought in the simple words: "In all things, not too much." Moderation as a requisite of philosophic enlightenment is a single word to cover a multitude of temperance's. Moderation, first of all, arises from an economy of resources, for in terms of energy, every intemperance is an extravagance. Most human beings die of their intemperance's, but not always from those familiar excesses which we associate with the word. Many people who eat moderately, drink not at all, and are apparently paragons of the virtues, die of intemperance. For example, intolerance is a form of intemperance, jealousy, worry, anger, fear—all these are intemperance's just as destructive and wasteful as the more familiar excesses of the flesh. Any unworthy, unbeautiful or uncontrolled waste of life, thought or feeling, is an intemperance. To do a disagreeable or injurious deed produces fully as destructive an effect on the soul as alcoholism or the drug habit, and all immoderation is habit-forming. Each time we lose our temper, it is more difficult to control it. Every excess leads to other excesses, and all excess destroys the beauty and symmetry of the soul's purposes. According to the teachings of occultism, the virtues have their origin in the understanding of the student himself. As a disciple becomes grounded in philosophy, he gradually becomes incapable of doing unphilosophic things. No one masters an evil habit until the habit itself falls away, because it is no longer consistent with the standard of living and thinking. The virtues

arise not from a desperate effort to inhibit the evil tendencies of the nature but rather from an unfolding inward beauty which, asserting itself, comes finally to dominate each action and render it likewise beautiful. Philosophy, by leading the mind away from excess, and establishing it firmly in moderate courses of thought and action, elevates the entire life, bestowing new inspiration and meaning upon each impulse and attitude. When the Golden Mean is established in men, the Golden Age will be established in the world.

6. DETACHMENT. Every man is ruled by that over which he exercises the sense of possession. Detachment is not only the mastery of the impulse to possess, it is the ability to disassociate values. For instance, the common attitude towards action and reward. It is unfortunately true that most people taking up the study of philosophy and the occult sciences are motivated by selfishness. The poor want to be rich, the sick want to be well, the humble want to be powerful and nearly all desire that their efforts should be rewarded in measurable, temporal terms. A great number turn to philosophy for consolation. Some in extremity grasp at wisdom as drowning men are said to grasp at straws. Religion is not a metaphysical breadline. All philosophers of merit and enlightenment have agreed that it is sacrilege to exploit the sacred teachings to accomplish those material ends which are entirely outside of the province of religion. By detachment in philosophy, we mean that every disciple worthy to receive instruction must come to the temple offering all that he has and all that he is for wisdom, expecting no other reward for his effort than wisdom. The philosopher desires wisdom above all the treasures of the earth because wisdom is necessary to the health of the soul and the perfection of the inner life, and this health and this perfection are necessary to the plan of human evolution. This wisdom and this perfection fulfill the destiny for which man was created. Man should no more be rewarded for trying to become wise than a child should be rewarded for growing up. The wider sphere of consciousness, the greater area of usefulness, the fuller measure of realization—these are the rewards of wisdom. They are not bestowed upon a man because he is wise, but the attainment of wisdom itself naturally produces these improvements in the consciousness. Strength is not given to a man as a reward for growing or as a reward for exercising—the means themselves produce the ends out of their own processes. There is a story frequently told of a Hindu chela who asked his master what a man had to do in order to become wise. The master took him into the Ganges and held the disciple's head under water

for several seconds. "What did you think of while I was holding your head down?" asked the teacher. "Only one thing," replied the chela, "I wanted air." "How badly did you want air?" "More than anything else in the world." "Did you think of wealth or rewards or ambitions?" "No master, only air." "Very well, my son, when you want wisdom as you just wanted air, then you will become wise."

7. RELAXATION. The achievement of philosophy is the most serious work in the world, but no one can afford to take it too seriously. One of the old poets has referred to the laughter of the gods on high Olympus, and I cannot but think sometimes that these gods are laughing a little at men who have forgotten how to laugh. All the great philosophers whose words and thoughts have survived the changes of time have possessed the sense of humor. It is observable that most students of metaphysics take themselves and their efforts too seriously for their own good and the comfort of others. Instead of mysticism bringing them a deep and abiding joy and peace, it bows them down with the weight of cosmos. It is perfectly possible to assume the moral responsibility for action and at the same time retain a native optimism and a sense of humor. It is always good for the young student to remember that, while the world and other people appear to be going to the dogs, this universe and all that it contains is really "going to heaven" as rapidly as it can. No one is failing. There are no lost souls. Although many seem to desire to grow by a difficult and unpleasant process—everyone is growing. Each individual is doing the best that he can for what he is and where he is, and as he becomes more, he will do better. Each individual should carry as heavy a burden as he can carry joyously, but when his morale begins to bend under the weight of his load, he is no longer contributing to the common good. The present financial depression has proved to thousands that happiness did not arise from possession but from values within the soul itself. This is an important lesson, worth all the sorrow that it has cost. In metaphysics, relaxation means even more than this detachment from strain and stress. It means the ability to rest the mind from the heavy processes of thinking by periodic detachment and repositing of the thinking process. Every human being, in order to be truly wise, must learn to play as well as work; It is very hard for serious-minded people to enjoy occupations of trivial importance, but the human brain is so constructed that it cannot stand constant strain for a protracted time. There must either be a let-down or a breakdown. The arts offer recreation to those whose minds are immersed in the sciences, and the sciences, in turn are necessary to those whose lives are given to the arts. Each life must have its vocation

and its avocation, and they should be sufficiently different that they bring completely different faculties into operation. An interesting book could profitably be written about the recreations of the great.

I cannot too strongly recommend relaxation to metaphysical students. Nearly all of those whom I have contacted in many years of public work have forgotten that philosophy is not only the science of living, but also the joy of living. We should all remember that if we do not live well in this world and appreciate the beauties of our present sphere, we shall scarcely merit a better world or a happier sphere.

At first these seven essential qualities may seem somewhat contradictory, but it must be remembered that it is the duty of the intelligent student to blend and balance what would otherwise be extreme courses of action. The blending of these seven qualities is the fine art of philosophy. He who completely accomplishes this blending is master of himself. Self-mastery leads to those higher ends of spiritual understanding to which all disciples aspire.

In next month's letter, we shall take up the seven requisites of the outer life which we have termed acquirements. The knowledge of certain arts and sciences is particularly useful in the understanding of occult philosophy. We shall consider these arts and sciences and explain why each of them makes a valuable contribution to the soul power of man.

* * * * *

QUESTION—Do disembodied spirits retain a memory of their earth-life experiences?

ANSWER—The simple experiments of spiritualism have demonstrated the continuity of consciousness beyond the grave, and all clairvoyants agree that a person who has passed from this state to the subjective plane retains identity and continues as the same individuality as during physical life. A man has four bodies making up what is termed the chain of his personality. The highest of these bodies is chemical organism. After physical death the individual functions briefly in his etheric double or vital body which also dies, never surviving for any considerable time the disintegration of the physical organism. Under normal conditions at this stage of our evolution, the average person functions for nearly a thousand years in the astral body. For this entire period, he retains the individuality of his previous incarnation. The astral body is then dissipated by a phenomenon resembling death and the consciousness is posited in its mental organism, in which it functions for a period of time consistent with its mental development. With the disintegration of the mental body, usually some twelve hundred years after death, the entity loses its individuality and becomes again a pure, spiritual principle. From this time, the memory of the past life exists only subjectively, and the continuity of consciousness is broken. Therefore, after the disintegration of the mental organism, the personality ends as such. This period is followed immediately by preparations within the ego itself for rebirth, when is causing a new personality to emerge out of its own potential creative power. There are some exceptions to this rule due to special developments. Very highly evolved entities will retain individual consciousness for a much greater time, but we should remember that it is not the personality that really grows. It is the ego, or inner self, growing through personality and using personality to the accomplishment of its own ends. Thus, John Doe, as a personality, does not grow through the ages; rather, the eternal Self or the spirit, causes a personality temporarily known as John Doe to be emanated out of itself. At the end of approximately twelve hundred years, John Doe is entirely reabsorbed into the spiritual cause from which it came, John Doe then absolutely ceases, but the experiences and characteristics of John Doe are incorporated into the consciousness of the permanent ego. Personalities are not reborn, but the principles behind personalities are constantly projecting personal organisms out of themselves and through these personal organisms contacting the experience spheres of life.

Yours very sincerely,

Manly P. Hall

LOS ANGELES, AUGUST 1, 1935

In last month's letter, we began a consideration of the fourteen requisites of the philosophic life. The seven requisites of the inner life, termed character, have already been outlined, so we shall now examine the seven requisites of the outer life, which we term Attainments.

It is often difficult for students to realize that the perfection of Self is the real-life work of each individual. The building of character, the unfolding of consciousness, the development of understanding—all these are processes which operate only under the direction of consecrated and enlightened will. Perfection is not a gift from the gods. Each person must work out his own salvation with diligence.

It was during those morbid centuries which we now term the "dark ages" that beauty and joy were excluded from the religious life. The doctrine that the material universe is a place of evil from which we should attempt a precipitous exit belongs to the same period of religious psychology. It is true philosophically that the material universe is impermanent and that it is wrong for the human soul to invest its hope of glory in material things. The wise of every generation have recognized the impermanence and insufficiency of temporal achievement. Yet this has not caused them to overlook the important lessons which physical life has to teach.

The most imminent of man's spiritual duties is the mastery of the physical environment wherein he has been placed by the lords of Karma. To evade the physical issues of life is to evade moral responsibility. The old teachings are very definite on this point. The ancient Mystery Schools permitted none to receive the esoteric tradition who had not perfected to at least a reasonable degree the conduct of the outer life. No reputable metaphysical system has ever encouraged individuals to pray, meditate, concentrate, visualize or affirm themselves out of those duties and obligations which form the motivating principle in material existence. This does not mean that metaphysical exercises do not have a place in the spiritual plan of life, but they are never to be regarded as substitutes for right action and intelligent thinking. It is quite evident that the initiates of the ancient world would not have demanded a high standard of excellence and ability from their disciples had not this standard been necessary to the understanding and application of the Wisdom Teachings.

It is therefore wise for every truth seeker to perfect himself in all useful lines of knowledge. We term the seven branches of essential knowledge Attainments because they are accomplished out of the effort and integrity of the individual. The purpose of all knowledge is the perfection of the soul—the soul being that part of man which transmutes experience into spiritual power. The experiences of the outer life feed the soul even as the impulses of the inner life nourish and sustain the objective personality. Olympiodorus in his banquet describes the feast of the soul, explaining that man very often feeds the body well but permits the soul to starve. From starvation, the soul dies or at least loses its power to influence the mind and heart. Now the food men eat does not retain its individuality but rather passes through certain chemical changes so that only a certain energy resident in it is finally assimilated into the human system. In the same way, knowledge, which man acquires does not retain its individuality in every case but, passing through an assimilative process in the consciousness, is transmuted into an energy which nourishes and perpetuates the soul. Thus, when men study music, art, literature, philosophy, or even the crafts it does not mean that the soul receives into itself a heterogeneous mass of ill-digested experiences, or that the soul merely becomes the image of the art or science that has been attained. A divine alchemy transmutes all experience and knowledge into a Hermetic medicine, the fabled panacea of the alchemists, that medicine which alone can cure ignorance—the disease of the uninformed.

It is not reasonable to expect each man to be master of all seven of the ancient sciences. In fact, at this stage of evolution it is a life work to achieve a reasonable degree of efficiency in one or two branches. Life is short and art is long, but the law of Reincarnation assures us that centuries of opportunity for accomplishment extend before us and that each life, if intelligently lived, contributes its part to the greater perfection which lies ahead of us.

Through the seven requisites of the inner life termed Character, we become capable of estimating deity as quality. Through the seven requisites of the outer life, Attainments, we gain the capacity to appreciate divinity as wisdom and activity. Of course, at the present time in our educational system, the metaphysical implications in the arts and sciences are denied or ignored. But this in no way detracts from the fact that these spiritual values exist. The arts and sciences, like most of the theologies of man, have been reduced to elements of an economic program, their esthetic factors sacrificed to the selfish institutions of man. Yet behind each art and science is a universal law and those who would discover the divine agent should not ignore the God who lives in His own works. The seven requisites which constitute the ancient outline of knowledge, the links of Homer's Golden Chain, are as follows:

1. MATHEMATICS. Under this heading are included the several departments of arithmetic, algebra, geometry, trigonometry, etc. Mathematics was cultivated by the earliest of civilized peoples. An exact knowledge of it is evidenced by architectural remains dating back to prehistoric times. Arithmetic is the science of exactness and bears witness to the consistency and immutability of law. The philosophical geometry of the Egyptians was the basis of Pythagorean philosophy. Plato was learned in the wisdom of Pythagoras and derived from this earlier teacher his celebrated axiom:

"God geometrizes." It is evident to the scientist that mathematics is not a man-made science but rather a discovery which man has made of a science which exists in the universe. A human being may possess a conscious knowledge of mathematical principles yet he shares this knowledge with the most minute creatures. The cell of the bee, the shell of the Radiolaria, and the geometrical form of the snowflake all bear witness to the universal arithmetic, a cosmic geometry.

Among mortals' mathematics is one of the driest of the sciences, but this is because an ignorant generation has divorced calculation from the drama of life. Most of the beauty that we see about us in nature is due to some aspect of cosmic arithmetic. We live in the midst of universal equations. Strangely enough, the study of mathematics is closely associated with the stimulation of intuition. Certainly, no person who has read the commentaries of Proclus on Euclid can fail to appreciate the sublimities of the numeral theory. Thousands of students seeking God in numerous metaphysical ways, by failing to master mathematics, have lost the opportunity of perceiving divinity manifesting itself through the glorious geometry of form.

2. ASTRONOMY. In olden times, what we term astronomy was embraced within the all-inclusive subject—astrology. No classical philosopher could have been interested in the arrangement of the sidereal bodies without instinctively desiring to understand the effect which these bodies produce upon man. Astrology is moral astronomy, and astronomy is astrology divorced from all practical purposes.

What use is it to know the number of the stars or to discover the elements of which they are composed, to measure their orbits and calculate the intensity of their light, if in the end we deny that any of these factors was in any way applicable to human existence? The first astronomers, from their high towers, established systems of time from the sidereal motions. From these have resulted calendars, most of which were originally devised for horoscopal purposes. Under the heading of astronomy is to be included the whole anatomy of the universe, the theories of history, the mysteries of climate and weather, the mutations of seasons which brings us naturally to agriculture and husbandry. In other words, astronomy was the orderer of life, one of the most civilizing of the sciences. To the mystic, astronomy is the key to magnitude values. Astronomy enlarges the universe, revealing a world too large for smallness, too glorious for meanness, too beautiful for hate, too honest for deceit. Astronomy reveals man's place in the plan. It shows him to be part of an infinity of incalculable life, and reveals the whole sidereal diffusion bound together by an all-ensouling wholeness. Man's kinship with the stars and the grain of sand is established.

3. BIOLOGY AND PHYSICS. These branches of learning gradually emerged from the alchemical researches of the ancient Chinese, Brahmins and Egyptians. The first practical laboratory was that part of the temple set aside for research in chemistry and medicine. The various branches of research in the chemical factors of life were not originally divided into numerous departments as now. Priests were the first scientists, the first physicians, and the first students of anatomy and physiology. We have listed these several sciences under one heading because they all directly or indirectly relate to structure and function. From these sciences, certain laws of nature become immediately evident. Man's exploration of nature and its processes gave rise to the theory of what we now call science. But in olden times, these researches were not carried on by scoffing materialists but by enlightened philosophers who discovered beneath the superficial aspects of form divine chemical and mechanical processes. Science is therefore the study of the anatomy of the body of God. The laboratory reveals not only the infinite mystery of life but also the infinite complexity of function. Man's veneration for the universal wisdom that supports this supreme order, sustaining all things in their proper relationships to all other things, grew with the increase of knowledge. Knowledge brings with it appreciation, and appreciation is one of the most beautiful forms of religion. Man is never far from a truth which he has learned to appreciate.

4. SOCIAL AND POLITICAL SCIENCE. This department of learning arose from man's contemplation of the motions and courses which are apparent in those social aggregates which we call nations and races. Included under the heading of social science was that vast body of tradition and research which has given rise to the laws governing relationships of individuals. The social sciences gave rise to the doctrines of morality and the various codes of convenience and compromise necessary to the survival of individuals under a social order. Therefore, we may consider with Cicero that civilization arises from the speculations of ancient wise men directed towards the improvement of community existence. Under the political sciences must be included government, leadership, and all regulation of community affairs by which the general motion and trend of empire is preserved towards those consistent ends for which empire was devised. Political science in the western worlds had its origin with Solon and received the refining influence of Plato and Aristotle. Statesmanship and political orga-

nization reached its height under the Romans with whom it also deteriorated into tyranny. Most modern governments are revivals of ancient policies, and the failure of the theory of government in the modern world is largely due to the increasing interval between natural law and political purpose. The statesmen of old were philosophers deriving their inspirations for government from astronomy, mathematics and physics. When political science divorced religion and philosophy, it lost the name of action. Governments, since that time, have never survived their own inherent weaknesses.

To the mystic the study of social and political science reveals both the strength and weakness of existing institutions, and prevents the earnest thinker from falling under the influence of traditional evils which have remained uncorrected since the decay of the religio-political institutions of antiquity.

5. MUSIC AND ART. Under this heading are included the numerous esthetic and cultural impulses which exist eternally in nature and have given rise to artistic institutions among men. Included with music and art are, of course, poetry, drama and the dance. The esthetic arts were all of religious origin, their development paralleling the unfolding of beauty in the human soul. To perfect oneself in an art is to feel a small part of that creative impulse by which the whole universe was brought out of chaos.

Beauty has always adorned truth. First, because truth moving through nature is eternally producing beautiful effects. Second, because men propitiating the universal good were inspired to perform their rites and rituals through beautiful institutions, symbolic of a divine beneficence. With the decline of classical civilization, man turned gradually from a religion of beauty to creeds of severity and melancholy. Several great nations completely destroyed their esthetic impulses by the experience of Puritanism which established vicious precedents which have impoverished national culture. In England for example, Puritanism practically destroyed music. The purity of religious arts has been perverted among nearly all modern peoples. From the esthetic arts, men learn to live beautifully and when these arts are explored to their divine origin, they inspire the human mind to nobler standards of action and relationship, bringing dignity and purpose to all the finest of human relationships. The arts feed the soul and soul starvation is responsible for much of the degeneracy and decadency which have perverted the esthetics of the present generation. The loss of art results in the loss of soul and the loss of soul in the end brings about the fall of empire.

6. LANGUAGE. Under the heading of language are included grammar and rhetoric, literature and the whole theory of the communication of ideas. The most ancient languages of the earth were mere sounds derived from nature by man seeking to express such primitive emotions as hope, despair, love, hate and fear. The history of language is a record of the gradual objectification of the subjective impulses of the human mind. Oral language gave rise gradually to hieroglyphics and written characters. Alphabets are conventionalized pictures devised by the progenitors of present races.

Language is the science of expression. He who expresses well shares himself with others. With our eyes, we may all perceive together some outer phenomenon of nature, but with our ears, we may listen to the thoughts of other men. We can hear their hopes, their dreams, and their aspirations, and we can share with them the fruits of our own experiences. The significance of language depends largely upon the meanings of words. Many of the greatest evils that have afflicted man have arisen from the misinterpretation of terms. This is particularly true in religion where numerous conflicting creeds have risen up to interpret in various ways the simple words of a single sentence. It is the purpose of words to communicate knowledge, thus increasing man's common share of truth, and enriching the life of each by the experience of others. Beautiful language has a ministry to perform and those who desire to serve truth and become part of the philosopher's hierarchy should equip themselves with the power of right expression. To study language is to find the universe in sounds, and the laws of life in the combinations of small symbolic figures called letters. The whole unity and diversity of existence is revealed in the mystery of alphabets. The evolution of language is as glorious a pageantry as the evolution of life.

7. PHILOSOPHY. The seventh place we have allotted to philosophy itself. Under this general heading, we include all man's groping for knowledge, by the laws of mind. The term philosophy was first used by Pythagoras to designate the science of the love of wisdom. Man, living in the midst of an infinite existence, reaches out from himself by intellectual extensions and seeks to grasp the whole of infinity within the narrow confines of his own intellect. Hence Philosophy. The mind being incapable of receiving and interpreting the infinities of the knowable, men of wisdom realized the necessity of exercising and developing the intellect itself, that its capacity to know and to retain knowledge might be increased.

Philosophy is more than merely thinking and arguing. It is the science of building up the capacity to know. Most people do not realize the limitations of their own thinking equipment.—They do not appreciate the years of preparation which must precede the capacity to understand. This preparation the old masters termed discipline. By discipline, they developed the numerous faculties of the thinking equipment until at last they gained the power to think God. By accomplishing this they liberated themselves forever from the superstitions of those who could not think God. Superstition brings truth down to the level of ignorance, clothing it in innumerable falsehoods. Philosophy elevates man to the level of truth, creating within him the capacity to sense and to realize, to visualize and to comprehend. For this reason, philosophers are termed the noblest race of men, for they alone perceive correctly the adequate reasons for the virtues of the race. To think is to wonder. To wonder is to discover. To discover is to know and to know is to be a philosopher.

* * * * *

QUESTIONS AND ANSWERS

QUESTION—Can the average individual control to any extent the length of time between incarnations or determine in advance what his next incarnation shall be?

ANSWER—Until an entity reaches a very high degree of spiritual development it does not have the power to control the intervals between incarnations. These intervals, like all other occurrences, arise from Karma. Normally speaking, the only way in which these intervals can be influenced is by the intensity of action, particularly mental action. We do not mean a mental effort to influence the time and condition of rebirth, but rather the general intensity of mental awareness. The more highly evolved the intellectual nature, the more profound and philosophic the thought, and the greater the scope of judgment, the longer will be the intervals between lives. This arises from the time required by the ego to assimilate into the soul nature the panorama of mental experience while on earth. Thus, the average individual can transmute the fruits of his mental activity into soul powers in a few hundred years of after death consciousness, but it is estimated that it will require ten thousand years for Plato to accomplish this, so great was his intellect. Therefore, unless Plato, being a very highly evolved soul, exercises his privilege as an adept to return sooner in the capacity of a teacher, he will normally remain out of incarnation for that length of time. As to the conditions of a future life, these cannot be directly influenced by the average person for the reason that the next incarnation may be devoted to working out the Karma of the present life or it may be dedicated to the transmutation of Karma brought forward from earlier incarnations but not included in the program of the present life. Of course, the whole future depends upon the increasing intelligence and integrity of present action.

QUESTION—If we do not develop spiritually in this life sufficiently to remember our past lives, do we automatically come into possession of this remembrance when we reach the astral world after death?

ANSWER—The transition between the material state and the after-death condition does not bring with it any major improvement in the degree of our knowledge or understanding. The astral body, in which we function after the decease of the physical organism, is not the depository of the records of past Karma. These records are preserved in the ego itself. The transition termed death, while it demonstrates to the individual himself the fact of immortality, it does not necessarily bring any broadened viewpoint on the fact of reincarnation and karma. Thus, spirit mediums seldom receive any instruction concerning rebirth from the discarnate entities that speak through them. The memory of past lives only comes to the individual when, he has reached a state of development by which the secrets which are locked in the consciousness itself are released into the sphere of objective thinking and knowing. The memory of past lives is locked within the superconscious Self. This Self is not released merely by dying, but only by the philosophical mystery commonly termed illumination.

QUESTION—Do parents give their children only physical bodies?

ANSWER—The old Wisdom Teachings reject what is commonly known as the law of heredity, explaining that the phenomena generally ascribed to heredity has its real source in reincarnation and Karma. By the law of attraction, the ego at birth is drawn into an environment similar to itself and suitable for the working out of its Karma. Thus, an entity whose Karma it is to suffer the experience of tuberculosis will be drawn into a tubercular family where it will receive a body susceptible to this disease. Science says that we do not inherit disease but a tendency to disease. Thus, parental environment and physical heredity are the instruments of the universal justice. Children resemble their parents in temperament because entities of similar temperaments incarnate in similar families and environments by the natural law that like attracts like.

QUESTION—Please differentiate between body, mind, soul, and spirit.

ANSWER—The term body should properly be applied to any one of the several vehicles of manifestation which the ego or Self emanates from its own being to serve as mediums of expression or function. The most generally recognized bodies in the case of man are the physical, vital, emotional, and mental. Bodies are not necessarily visible, nor are they always tangible to any physical sense perception. To use Plato's simple definition: A body is any structure or form to which energy is communicated.

MIND is variously defined in different schools of metaphysics. It is most generally accepted as the coordinated sublimation of bodily impulses. In other words, it represents the sum of the numerous instincts and impulses enlivened or quickened by d ray of rational energy from what the ancients termed the Self or the spiritual Over-Being from which personality is suspended. Mind is the mediator between spirit and body, referred to as the common ground. The position which the mind occupies in man—half way between invisible cause and visible effect—has given rise to nearly all the Messianic religious doctrines of the world. In several schools of philosophy, the Messiah is an enlightened mind which finally lifts the personality to truth through its own nature.

SOUL is a very loosely used, term and the indiscriminate misapplication of terms causes endless confusion among the schools of metaphysics. Soul is generally regarded as synonymous with spirit, but the ancient's regarded soul as an intuitional body built up in man by the assimilation of experience. All men perform good and evil deeds. These actions give rise to experience, and experience justifies action. No matter how much a man may suffer, if this suffering results in experience, it is always worth all it costs. Soul is the spiritual gold arising from the transmutation of the baser instincts and emotions. In the ancient Mysteries, the soul is termed the "robe of glory." It is the spotless, seamless garment of transmuted emotion, thought and action which each disciple of truth must wear when he seeks admission to the Hidden House.

SPIRIT to the ancients meant life. Not life in its physical aspect of vitality, but rather that universal life principle which pervades, animates, and sustains existence. Specifically, the term is applied to the causal substance in man, the abstract life energy, the abiding reality in the midst of ever-changing appearances. To the eastern philosopher spirit is never regarded as individualized. One man does not have one spirit and another man, another spirit. Spirit is universal. All diversity ends in spirit, and spirit is never divided. Thus, men are an innumerable race of personalities divided in form, indivisible in spirit.

QUESTION—Is a balance between introversion and extroversion better than introversion even though the latter is associated with serious thought but no social contact?

ANSWER—This is a psychological question involving factors little understood by even the most advanced psychologist. Introversion or the subjectification of action is a retiring from the circumference to the center of action. Except in rare cases, introversion results in inhibition and inhibitions lead to most of the evils which afflict the metaphysically minded. On the other hand, extroversion—the complete objectification of self—is the phenomenon of energies rushing constantly from a center to the circumference. In introversion, there is not enough expression and in extroversion, there is not enough control. It is the constant duty of the wise man to preserve a balance between expression and control. Introversion is one of the most common diseases of the learned, and extroversion is the plague of the uninformed. Men who thinly much do little, and with much action there is usually small thought. To bind each action to an adequate reason and to visualize each thought as manifesting in an appropriate consequence is to keep open and well-regulated the courses of energy in the human consciousness. A serious thinker must think seriously concerning the application of his thoughts to their reasonable ends in action. To think constantly and do nothing is not the way to become wise. To weary the faculties with constant strain and never rest them through proper relaxation from mental effort is to endanger the reason and impair the health. A well-balanced thinker always has a proper relaxation and strives to prevent a narrowness of viewpoint by keeping in reasonably close contact at all times with other persons of different thoughts and ideas. Such a procedure will, in the long run, contribute more to the philosophy itself than constant application to abstractions.

QUESTION—What is the most useful thing in this world?

ANSWER—Many people will differ in answering this question. Some might say electricity, others printing, others the telephone. Probably no better answer to this question can be found than that which Thales gave to the Pharaoh of Egypt. The great Greek sophist said: Virtue is the most useful thing in the world, for by the presence of it all other things are made beautiful and good, and without it even the most spectacular accomplishment is hurtful and incomplete.

QUESTION—Will the finality of life ever be known?

ANSWER—It is difficult for a person who is part of a forever growing universe to even think in terms of finality. Ultimates are dangerous thoughts. They are intellectual barriers to those realizations of infinity, which are natural to the inner life of man. Mem reaches finality by becoming finality, for all ultimates are God. Man is as far from ultimates as he is from absolute divinity. The philosophers conceive no static states beyond action. To the Buddhist that Nirvana which is the end of finites is merely the beginning of infinites. When men grow too wise to be men, they become ever-growing wisdom. Occasionally, we meet metaphysicians who suffer from the delusion that they will speedily achieve to the end of all human seeking and will repose individually in the perfection of ultimate accomplishment. These poor souls have been deluded either by themselves or by others. In the words of the old teaching, "life is ever becoming, but it never becomes."

QUESTION—If we are to do good, does it matter if we hurt people's feelings doing it?

ANSWER—This question reminds me of an old friend, a Methodist minister, whose motto was, "If I don't hurt somebody's feelings, I'm not preaching the gospel." Seriously speaking, the whole answer to this question depends upon the interpretation of the word good. There are two kinds of illusionary good—my good and the other fellow's good. Both of these are often at direct variance with that universal good which done is red. To do good is a fine art and those who dabble in reform without a depth of wisdom, of vast tolerance, and great experience in life, often do more harm than good. It is true that we are to do good, but it is also true that we are to become wise, and it is proven by experience that only those who are wise can really do good. When action is dominated by opinions or selfishness or sympathy or any emotion or thought that is not grounded in actual fact, our efforts to do good usually lose the name of action. It is well to bear in mind in our efforts to do good the Socratic definition of this virtue. "That which is true, necessary and beautiful is good." Our most common mistake in attempting to do good is to overlook the factor of beauty in action. That is why we are lively to hurt people's feelings. Others often are not as offended by what is said as by the way it is said. There are beautiful ways to do everything and they are usually acceptable. But when beauty fails in the deed, the deed itself usually misses its mark. Beauty is not weakness or sentiment; it is the divinity in the deed. Nowhere is beauty more needed in action than in reforms and corrections, and there is nowhere where it is less lively to appear. It is true we are all here to do good, but if we do not wish our ministrations to inadvertently contribute to the world's evils, our labors must reflect the beauty and understanding which we have developed within ourselves.

QUESTION—In what way does Rosicrucianism differ from other Wisdom Religions and when did it have its beginning?

ANSWER—Rosicrucianism, as it is now popularly taught, is an interpretation of the old Mystery Teachings in the light of Christianity. It therefore differs from all pre-Christian movements and from the occult schools of non-Christian peoples, principally in its interpretation of the significance of Christ. To the ancient pagans and to the non Christians of the modern world, Christ is either a universal principle independent of time and place, or else the Messianic attributes are bestowed upon the prophets or leaders of other faiths. The Rosicrucianism of the seventeenth century was a philosophical, rather than a religious movement. Its members were Cabalists, Alchemists, Hermetists, astrologers, and disciples of the transcendental arts, but when called upon to make a declaration of their faith the members of the original Society acknowledged allegiance to the Lutheran Church in Germany or the Reformed Church of England. The Rosicrucian Society is popularly supposed to have been founded about the year 1610 by a German Lutheran theologian, Johann Valentin Andrea. Our researches incline us to believe that the Society was actually founded about 1604, probably by Lord Bacon, and was composed of such disciples and initiates of the old Hermetic mysteries as had survived the Inquisition in Europe. The story of Christian Rosenkreutz is probably allegorical, as he is not even mentioned by several of the earliest historians of the Order.

Yours sincerely,

Manly P. Hall

944 West 20th Street.
Los Angeles, Calif.

LOS ANGELES, SEPTEMBER 1, 1935

QUESTION—There are many different schools of mysticism and occultism in the world. How can a student discover with certainty the system best suited to his individual needs?

ANSWER—Philosophic religion has existed among men from the earliest recorded periods. No age has been without a spiritual revelation sufficient to its needs, no race has been left godless, and no nation has risen to power without religious institutions flourishing in its midst. The religious instinct is one of those fundamental impulses which all men share together, and the history of religion is in substance the history of civilization itself. Nor have the fundamental principles of religious life and purpose been greatly modified by the passing of centuries. True, the more barbarous practices of savage peoples have been modified by the cultural impulses which have developed in the race. But the essential values of the religious factor in individual and collective existence remain practically unchanged. The theories of religion in vogue today are the same theories which governed spiritual institutions of the ancient world. Therefore, we may properly interpret the needs of the modern truth seeker in the light of those codes and principles which have survived the vicissitudes of countless ages.

Certain facts have been justified by the experience of ages. Chief of these facts is the inevitable inequalities which exist in the reasoning capacities of men. There has never been a time in recorded history when the inhabitants of even one community were all of equal spiritual achievement. The severed races which together inhabit the earth constitute an innumerable inequality of abilities. The social systems which exist within races or form parts of nations and communities are themselves divided into numerous strata according to the mental, spiritual and physical differences which are present throughout humanity. In all times then, and among all peoples there are few capable of great perfection of thought and action, and the vast majority is lacking in the capacity for exact and inspired thinking. It has always been necessary, therefore, to consider these inequalities when founding or promulgating a religious doctrine. This condition, beyond immediate remedy by man, has forced religious and philosophical systems to grade their teachings, presenting only the simplest part of their doctrine to those of immature intellect, and reserving the most profound of their wisdom for the discerning and qualified few. If we realize with St. Paul that all men are not equally qualified to receive those esoteric traditions which are the very soul and substance of religion, we can understand the origin of those numerous cults which must inevitably spring up to serve the spiritual needs of a greatly diversified humankind. There must be "milk for babes" and "meat for men." There must be simple revelations suitable to minister to the needs of the spiritual peasantry, and more complicated and profound traditions to satisfy the mature thinking of enlightened persons. There is no evil in a diversity of cults; the evil arises from the failure of these cults to realize that they are all part of one spiritual program.

There has never been but one religion among men, but this religion, which Mohammed termed the natural faith of mankind, has been variously interpreted by various peoples in various ages. In recent times these various interpretations have lost the realization of their final identity and have come to regard themselves as superior and distinct revelations. From this error has arisen the competitive theory which has unfortunately permeated most of the religious institutions of the earth. The result has been a confusion of tongues and the phenomena of hundreds, yes thousands, of religious sects and isms laboring under the delusion of difference, each claiming superiority over the others, and attempting to discredit the tenets of all cults save its own.

The enlightened student of metaphysics who has come to realize the fundamental unity of all life and purpose is not to be deceived by the contention of factions but recognizes all the faiths of man as fragments of a universal religion which is part of the very existence of all living things. Freed, therefore, from an unphilosophical addiction to creeds and dogmas, the honest and earnest seeker after the spiritual truths of life can examine dispassionately all beliefs and can claim as his own the good which he finds in each. Thus, we may pass over the issue of religious authority and, with an enlightened tolerance towards the beliefs of all men, examine the second factor in our problem.

The great religious systems of the ancient world, which have descended to us as the bases of our present beliefs, were greatly influenced by the factors of race geography. Race determined the profundity of the revelation and geography influenced its symbolism and interpretation. Races are the rung-levels on the ladder of evolution and each race is divided into sub-races, which represent quality levels within the racial structure itself. No two types or clans or communities in the world today are on precisely the same level of evolution. Each of the material divisions of the social system represents a level of unfolding consciousness, and furnishes an environment for the attainment of certain vital experiences necessary to the final perfection of man. It naturally follows that souls evolving in each of these levels must have a spiritual interpretation of life suitable to the experiences of these levels. This is one of the reasons why missionary activities are so generally unsuccessful. It is profitless, yes finally impossible, to convert any man to a spiritual code beyond his awareness or inconsistent with his present cycle of experience. Missions have therefore succeeded where they ministered to health or carried on educational work, but when they seek to deflect the individual from the course of his own consciousness, they accomplish more harm than good.

Each of the great racial divisions of mankind received at its inception an interpretation of religion consistent with the purpose of the racial consciousness. These revelations were all derived from the same ancient and ageless source that we may term for practical purposes the Wisdom Religion of the world. Not only did each race receive its own tradition but each race as it unfolded developed and specialized its tradition until the racial faiths took on distinct individualities. It is these individualities, now for the most part crystallized and inflexible, which we term the religious systems of the world. To classify a few of them:

1. BRAHMANISM. This was the religious system of the primitive Aryans, built up from a tradition which has been individualizing for nearly a million years. Brahmanism is the fundamental religious impulse of India and has gradually been broken up into numerous dependent systems such as Yoga, Vedanta and Tantric philosophy.

2. CONFUCIANISM. This is really the comparatively modern crystallization of the ancient traditions of the Atlantean Chinese, reformed and restated by the great philosopher Confucius. Numerous Chinese sects are derived from the fundamental tenets of Confucian authority.

3. TAOISM. This philosophy, which also developed in the Chinese racial consciousness, represents one of the migrations of Brahminic philosophy, thus mingling with Chinese thought, this Hindu tradition, ministered to a certain level in the unfolding Mongolian consciousness.

4. ZOROASTRIANISM. Several prophets known by the name of Zoroaster rose up to minister to the spiritual needs of the Irano-Aryan migrations. As the Persian civilization rose, the Magian cult of Zoroaster came to power

and was finally reformed and restated some 600 years before the Christian era by Spitama, the last of the Zoroaster's. Under the name Mithraic the Persian cults reached Rome to serve a certain level of Roman thought, and finally the Persian stream mingled with the waters of Christianity.

5. BUDDHISM. This ancient faith, also rising in India, was one of the first to branch off from the Brahminic tree. It retained individuality for thousands of years, to finally emerge as a great world religion about B.C. 500 under the leadership of Gautama Buddha. Buddhism broke into several parts, migrated to most of the Eastern nations, where its influence has been felt from Ceylon and Java on the South to Tibet and Japan on the North.

6. THE ORPHIC THEOGONY. This philosophic system, also a branch of the Brahminic tree, developed in the classical civilizations of the Near East, becoming the spiritual power behind the cultural supremacy of the Greeks. Orphic philosophy was revealed by Orpheus, Pythagoras and Plato, and mingled with the Mithraic in Rome, the Egyptian Mysteries in Egypt, and also Christianity. This mingling resulted in Gnosticism, and also influenced Jewish metaphysics through the Essene and Nazarene sects.

7. OSIRIS WORSHIP. Also of Eastern origin, this faith was successfully transplanted to Egypt where it flourished for more than 5000 years and finally disintegrated with the collapse of Egyptian culture, and continues now only as an impulse in Christian thought.

8. JUDAISM. Technically speaking we must accept Judaism as rising among the Egyptian, Chaldean and other ancient peoples in the Mesopotamian area. Under the leadership of Moses, the great migration of the Jewish nation took place which finally individualized the faith which has continued to the present time with very few modifications.

9. CHRISTIANITY. The decadence of the pagan mysteries, due to the demoralizing effect of the disintegration of old peoples and the military era inaugurated by Rome, necessitated a restatement of the Wisdom Religion some 2000 years ago. This restatement, under the name of Christianity, constitutes the spiritual urge behind the development of the European and American culture.

10. MOHAMMEDANISM. The last of the great world religions to come into being was the faith of Islam, the strongest branch to come from the tree of primitive Christianity. From the sixth century A.D. on Islamism has increased in strength, and at the present time represents the most powerful rival to Christianity in the religious world. It has converted most of the

Near East and penetrated far into Asia. Strangely enough, in the form of Islamism, some of the earliest of the Brahminic theological doctrines return as a stranger to their own country.

In addition to this panorama of religious motion in the world, it is necessary to recognize the numerous cults which have sprung up combining factors from two or more of the great religious movements. These major schools have been subject to innumerable reformations and their doctrines to numerous interpretations and reinterpretations. To the average person of the Western World Christianity is the familiar example of religious growth. The hundreds of sects which have sprung up in this religion alone are typical of similar divisions existing in other world faiths. Each of these sects claims precedence over the others for accuracy of interpretation, and sublimity of purpose. It is not surprising, therefore, that the layman in religious matters, when confronted with the complexity everywhere present in matters of faith, should wonder which way to turn in order to secure spiritual knowledge in its most nearly pure and unadulterated form.

But even this picture of existing conditions is not the whole of the story. There is yet a third factor to be considered, and this is the individual truth seeker himself. Although today millions of persons are born together in a great nation like America, they should in no way be regarded as similar in capacity or interests merely because of the circumstance of birth. This country, but a few centuries old, has received into it egos whose previous lives have taken place in numerous other civilizations, and who bring with them religious impulses and spiritual predilections from all the great faiths of the ancient world. Five sons born into one family may have locked within their subconscious selves the religious convictions of five different world religions. These differences are plainly evident to the trained observer and very often have stamped themselves upon the appearance of the individual. Thus, children born of centuries of Anglo-Saxon ancestry may have about them the impression that they have come from some far Eastern country.

Therefore, side by side in any gathering of hundred percent Americans are souls whose spiritual experiences bind them with the faiths and cultures of the world's most distant places. A man may be born an American and yet be, by spiritual thought and moral code, a Greek, a Brahman, a Buddhist or a Mohammedan.

In harmony with the consistent course of Western life, all these people may be nominally members of the Christian faith in this present life. But a man, though christened a Baptist here, remains religiously what his soul is. If in previous lives he has been a Brahman, he is bound to interpret Christianity in terms of Brahminic philosophy. A good example of a Western man with an Eastern soul is America's one great philosopher, Ralph Waldo Emerson. When, therefore, a person living in this century, in this civilization, asks the question—what are my spiritual needs?—it is a large matter to decide this. It is impossible to establish an interpretation of religion which suits the needs of all people because these people bring with them out of the deathless past impulses and attitudes which must be ministered to individually and intelligently. This explains the reason why many faiths and many interpretations flourish together among nearly all progressive peoples. Here also is revealed the absurdity of attempting to establish state faiths and creeds or to regiment human religious instincts. This is also the reason why each truth seeker, in his search among faiths for the solution to his problem, finds at last someone believes that more than any other is suitable to his needs.

Having thus traced the general course of our problem, we must next examine what may be termed the anatomy and physiology of religion. It was customary among the enlightened theologies of antiquity to distinguish grades of interpretation suitable for the numerous classes which exist within any society. From this comes the fashion of dividing all religious instructions into two general parts, termed exoteric and esoteric. This division was, not arbitrarily determined by the priesthood but arose from a phenomenon evident everywhere in society. The majority of humankind are incapable of understanding, applying or appreciating the more profound aspects of a philosophical religion. Thus, faiths were simplified to human need. The great body of each religious system consisted principally of moral doctrines, commandments and injunctions to propriety and honesty. These simple codes regulated the body of society and gave ordinary persons a protective character-building code of life. The Golden Rule became the standard of human relationships in over forty great faiths, nor can any man deny today that this code, if applied, would solve most of the problems of empire. Nor can any man hope to ascend to the higher mysteries of spiritual existence who has not mastered and applied this simple formula of integrity. The majority of humanity neither questions nor enquires beyond the narrow circumference of creature comforts. To live honestly and comfortably and to die with the hope that the future will prove benevolent approximately epitomizes the spiritual problems of the multitude. In fact, many well-educated and informed persons believe that this is all the religious knowledge that any human being needs and that all the rest is fancy and illusion. There is always, however, a certain class in society not so easily satisfied. These demand a more inclusive and mature religious understanding. They perceive, even though but dimly, that the spiritual problem of life is far greater than merely a moral code. This does not mean that they reject the simple truths of honesty and right living, but rather that out of ages of evolution, the soul within has come to realize that life is not a material but a spiritual experience. Religion is not merely a part of existence, a series of arbitrary moral codes. Religion is the whole of existence. Spiritual facts are the only facts and the whole material universe is merely a tiny spiritual particle vibrating in a vast measureless, unknowable sea of spirit. This realization brings with it an irresistible desire to investigate the divine world which surrounds and interpenetrates what we have come to call the material world.

This impulse to spiritual investigation comes only to the soul somewhat matured in spiritual values. History records that these truth seekers have existed in every civilization. They have always been in the minority as to members but they have been pioneers of progress and most of the world's advancement in fineness and character has been due to their efforts and their ideals.

What we term a truth seeker today is one of this small group who, dissatisfied with physical existence even under moral law, desires to explore and understand the worlds of mind and soul and spirit extending beyond the limits of our material perceptions. It was for these more advanced types that the esoteric doctrines of the ancients were evolved, and an inner tradition suitable to the needs of these advanced types is present in the structure of every great religion. All faiths have their inner or esoteric schools into which they accept as students those who have outgrown the outer and more evident interpretations of religious knowledge. The Brahmins had their Mystery Temples at Ellora and Elephanta. The Egyptians had their crypts of initiation under the Island of Philae. The Buddhists established their Mystery School in the Saptaparna Caverns even during the time of Gautama. All the great world religions, though divided by the superficial differences of their exoteric creeds, unite in their esoteric knowledge. It is this Secret Doctrine which all the faiths of the world share in common that interests all sincere students of religion. The quest of essential wisdom is the great work of life. In our letter next month, we shall a-tempt to set forth certain simple rules and directions which will help students in determining the path to truth most suitable to them.

* * * * *

QUESTION—Please give your version of the idea of a person being divinely protected. We so often hear someone say that they have no fear of anything because they are divinely protected. Does not the law of cause-and-effect render this idea untenable?

ANSWER—Most exponents of the cult of "divine protection" derive their ideas from one of several systems of mental metaphysics which seek to make man right with his world by surrounding him with a wall of mental or autosuggestions. It would be folly to deny that mental attitude is capable of producing a marked effect upon the external life of the individual, but effects that are inconsistent with the spiritual facts of the individual's life are impermanent and consistently disastrous. All enlightened systems of philosophy and mysticism agree that it is impossible in the long run to fool the law of cause and effect. If by mental processes we attract to ourselves things which are not our own by merit, our very possessions become our misery and everything we gain is a loss to ourselves. No person under any condition can be divinely protected from the effects which he has set in motion by his own causations. He may build a mental wall of defense by which he temporarily deflects the thunderbolts of Karma but this is not divine protection—this is mortal will, defying divinity. In the old fables, mortal will under the name of Satan and his angels defies the edict of heaven and sets up its kingdom in the Abyss. Mental metaphysicians have much in common with the fallen angel. When we resist that which we have caused to come to us, when we refuse to acknowledge the debts which we have made, when we surround ourselves with a wall of mental electricity, we are not divinely protected—we are simply resisting for a little while those consequences which must ultimately catch up with us. Worse than this, our attitude towards destiny being wrong, we usually are extravagant in our desires and unreasonable in our attitudes, thus bringing the sum of our debts much higher than it would normally be. The only protection with which we can safely surround ourselves is the invincible armor of our own integrity. Man is not protected by the gods but by the honor that is within him.

QUESTION—Please give the names of the best worlds to read on the interpretation of the Grecian myths.

ANSWER—The mythological writings of the Greeks are founded for the most part upon the secret traditions of the Orphics. According to the old records, Orpheus, whose name means "dark of skin" brought the ancient Wisdom Religion from India to the progenitors of the classical Hellenes. It is impossible to interpret Greek mythology philosophically without the Orphic keys. The writings of Homer and Hesiod were derived from the initiation pageantry of the Orphic cult, perpetuated in the Eleusinian and Dionysian Mysteries. Books dealing with this obscure subject in an enlightened manner are few and for the most part rare. Of particular importance are the translations and writings of Thomas Taylor, the Platonist. His mystical hymns of Orpheus is important, also his dissertation ON THE ELEUSINIAN AND BACCHIC MYSTERIES, and his essay on the odyssey of homer which serves as an appendix to his translations of the four books of Plotinus on abstinence from animal food. Of more recent writers, probably the most reliable is G. R. S. Mead, whose splendid little work Orpheus is derived in some parts from original Greek sources. In other parts, it is a summary of Thomas Taylor's researches.

QUESTION—Has the sixth root race started to appear upon the earth?

ANSWER—According to the metaphysical philosophy of the Brahmins, human life upon the earth manifests through seven out-pourings which are called races. The first of these races is called the Polarian and inhabited a vast polar continent hundreds of millions of years ago. The second was the Hyperborean, referred to by the Greeks as a semidivine race dwelling in the land north of the winds. The third was the Lemurian, a dark civilization existing upon a continent involving what is now the Indian Ocean and the Australasian Archipelago. The fourth was the Atlantean whose great island continent filled a considerable part of what is now called the Atlantic Ocean, extending from Greenland on the North to a southern latitude approximately parallel with Brazil. The fifth, to which we now belong, is called the Aryan and had its origin in North Central Asia about a million years ago. The sixth and seventh races are yet to come. The sixth race will be derived from the highest types produced by the fifth race and may spring up among several progressive peoples simultaneously. The application of the term "sixth root race" personality to describe a precocious or unusual type of human being is a figure of speech rather than a scientific fact. I question very much if true sixth root race types are as yet appearing, as many thousands of years must pass before the advent of the sixth race. It is quite possible however that tendencies which will later develop into sixth root race qualities are beginning to appear as progressive impulses in our present society. Some believe that the sixth root race will emerge from the chemistry of inter-racial minglings in America. Others feel that Russia is the logical cradle inasmuch as great social experiments are being carried on there. Australia has also been advanced as a possible field for sixth root race activities. It is my opinion that pioneers from the several subdivisions of our present race will form the nucleus for the future human type and that when the time comes for the sixth race to be objectified from the physical world a new continent will rise, probably in the Pacific Ocean, to serve as a theater of action for the new race.

QUESTION—Please give a practical definition of mysticism.

ANSWER—There are three terms in common use among metaphysicians which should receive an exact definition. Exoterically speaking, occultism is the intellectual approach to truth; mysticism is the emotional approach to truth; and psychism is the physical approach to truth. Esoterically, the occultist desires to possess wisdom; the mystic desires to be possessed by wisdom; and the psychic, incapable of impersonating wisdom, seeks to achieve a spiritual state by permitting his own metaphysical organisms to be controlled by other entities, by this process hoping to benefit by the experience of others. Practical mysticism may be defined as the intuitional grasp of reality. The practical mystic is one whose outer life is regulated by the beauty, gentleness and sublimity of inward conviction. Mysticism is the sublimation of emotion. The Buddhist would define it as the transmutation of passions into compassions, the elevation of attachments from a level of particulars to the level of impersonals.

QUESTION—The expectation of the coming of a World Teacher seems to be widespread, being as common in Asia, for example, as in this country. Is there a justification for this expectation?

ANSWER—Among the better-informed students of the esoteric traditions, there is no immediate expectation of the advent of a World Teacher. This does not mean that heroic personalities will not appear to aid the progress of the race. There is seldom a time when emissaries of the Great School are not at work in the world. The fifth race, our race, has already received its spiritual revelation, and no other major revelation can be expected until we have applied the wisdom that has already been given to us. About the year 1975, the next emissary of the Great White Lodge is expected but this representative will not be regarded as a World Teacher but merely as one of a long line of instructors who appear in the closing quarter of each century.

The Lord Maitreya, who's coming is awaited in Asia, and who, in terms of Tibetan metaphysics, has already "lowered one foot from his throne of the golden lotus," will be the World Teacher of the sixth root race and his coming cannot be expected until the nucleus of the sixth root race is fairly well integrated. In the meantime, disciples of the Ancient Wisdom receive their instruction from the "ever-coming Lord" within themselves.

QUESTION—What part does nationality play in Reincarnation? Does a person incarnate into a different nation each time he is reborn?

ANSWER—For practical purposes we may regard nations as parts of races. They are rungs in the ladder of racial evolution. Nations offer specialized environments for the lives evolving within a racial consciousness. The nation into which an individual is born is determined by evolution and Karma. The ego is not necessarily reborn each time into a different nation. It often requires many lives to outgrow national environments. National consciousness can hold egos to national programs for several lives. The present tendency towards internationalism is reflected in the short lives of nations, whereas ancient national institutions used to exist for thousands of years. Few nations today retain their essential characteristics for more than from three hundred to five hundred years. This itself is an indication of the speeding up of evolution, a tendency consistent throughout nature. As consciousness unfolds, nationalism must give way to internationalism, and evolution itself will finally bring about the condition of men living together in equity and peace.

QUESTION—Please tell us what sorcery really is?

ANSWER—Sorcery is black magic. In the ancient Atlantean world, a division took place in the occult arts. This resulted in what was called the two paths—white and black magic. White magicians were designated Masters of the Right, and black magicians Masters of the Left. The difference between white and black magic is essentially the difference in motive. White magic is founded upon unselfishness, black magic upon selfishness, and a student of the Ancient Wisdom is white or black according to the merit of the impulse which urges him to accomplishment and action. Sorcery is the use of occult knowledge for selfish personal purposes at the expense of others. When we use superior wisdom to gain advantage over those more ignorant than we are, then we are sorcerers. When we use superior knowledge to aid and perfect others, then we are white magicians. There is a third term—natural magic—that is used by aboriginal peoples who are able to control the elements of nature, as in the causing of rain, the practices of the medicine man, and the Shaman Natural magic, like the marvels of science, is impersonal, but the moment moral factors are involved, it becomes white or black according to its constructive or destructive use. Metaphysics today has in its ranks thousands of little parlor sorcerers—"thinking prosperity" meditating for power, and scheming occultly for superiority over each other.

QUESTION—Are there any other records of Jesus than the four Gospels?

ANSWER—The principal sources of information concerning the life and teachings of Jesus are the four so-called Gospels. In addition to these records there are Apocryphal Gospels, still regarded as uncanonical, containing fragments of history and some material evidently legendary. The Jewish Talmud mentions a Jesus who preached and healed in Nazareth and Galilee, and was stoned to death for his heresies. It would seem however that the Jesus of the Talmud (Jehoshua) lived about 100 B.C. The writings of the ante-Nicaean fathers contain some traditions presumably derived from first century sources. The most important of the ante-Nicaean records are found in Irenaeus. There is a brief statement in Josephus, but this is regarded by most authors as a forgery. Fragmentary mentions of Jesus are to be found in many third and fourth century Christian documents, but he is ignored by all the important historians of his time. Taking it all in all, the Gospels remain as the only systematic exposition of his life and works. The most important records outside of the Gospels are the Gnostic writings, but in these Christ is treated as symbolical rather than historical, and they are not contemporary.

QUESTION—What is the best way to overcome an obsession?

ANSWER—The word obsession has two meanings at the present time. Occultly speaking, an obsession is a form of possession in which a living person is overshadowed or dominated by the intelligence of another entity. Most often the other entity is discarnate. Psychologically speaking, an obsession is a fixation in which the natural flow of the intellect is deflected or perverted by some idea or notion which has come to dominate the reasoning processes. In the case of true obsession, it is my observation that certain physical derangements are usually present. Persons of normal mental attitudes, well directed emotions and healthy physical bodies are seldom obsessed. Obsessions most generally occur as the result of dabbling in occult sciences, years of emotional excess or repression, and a condition of anemia in the body chemistry. It follows that if the obsessed person has periods of lucidity and self-control, they should be set to work normalizing their lives. Where the obsession is continuous and the patient can offer no personal assistance, those treating the obsession must do everything possible to normalize the patient without his assistance. The resistance of the physical body must be brought up, but at the same time it is dangerous to feed an obsessed person animal food. Obsessing entities are usually of a lower moral and mental caliber than the person whom they attack but in order for the obsession to continue there must be a negative link of sympathy between the entity obsessing and the person obsessed. This link of sympathy must be sought for and removed. A serious case of obsession will not generally respond to amateur treatment, but must be worked on by a person experienced in occult therapeutics. Mild cases arising from mediumship can generally be remedied by the sufferer himself if he will reorganize his spiritual life and place it on a strong individual foundation. Thought power is a great force in working with obsessions and constructive thought regularly directed to the sufferer by a group of sympathetic people has been known to work wonders. In no case, however, should these thought impulses be sent forth in a destructive way even against the obsessing entity, for we do not fight evil with evil, but evil with good.

Yours very sincerely,
Manly P. Hall

LOS ANGELES, OCTOBER 1, 1935

Dear Friend,

One of the greatest problems in modern mystical philosophy is to free the popular mind from the conceit that a little metaphysical speculation relieves the individual from all responsibility and duties of the temporal state. Self-improvement is one of the first duties of man, for only through ages of Self-improvement can we achieve to that state of wisdom we so greatly desire. The practice of mysticism is not a substitute for improvement nor does it bestow upon us any knowledge or skill in those exact arts and sciences, the mastery of which is necessary to our spiritual security.

Some will say that a mastery of material arts can have little meaning to the spiritual man, for, like other aspects of illusionary existence, these arts must finally be dissipated by the light of perfect reason. It is unquestionably true that all human institutions are so full of ignorance and imperfection that, in terms of ultimates, they are of but passing moment, yet the mastery of these arts and sciences is of greater account than may first appear. The first merit of learning is discipline. The integrity by which an individual remains faithful to a certain line of effort is itself a vital factor in soul growth. You may well say that they do not speak Greek in heaven, so why should we learn it on earth? The answer to this is that it is not the Greek, which is learned, but the ability to learn Greek and the strength and specialization of faculties that is important. In the same way, we study many things here that are of no use hereafter. They are necessary here and excellence in them is a vital factor in our well-being hereafter.

To the mystic material, knowledge may seem to be a mass of trifles. But, as Michaelangelo said, "trifles make perfection and perfection is no trifle." The thousands of experiences of our material existence may seem in themselves insignificant but together they make up the perfection of action, and this perfection is the foundation of our divine existence. Let all serious thinkers remember that material existence, with its confusions and discords, is part of the divine plan, and being part of the plan, is evidently necessary to those creatures which are evolving through it. If we were not supposed to master the physical world, we would not be placed here nor does philosophy allow that being here our first impulse should be to escape. Rather, we should realize that only those who are faithful unto little things shall be made master over greater things. If we cannot live in this small part of the universe, how can we become citizens of a greater world with vaster and more numerous complexities.

As an excuse for lack of knowledge and lack of incentive to learn, a certain class of metaphysicians affirm, upon the authority of the Bible, that if they seek first the kingdom of heaven, all else will be added unto them. Or possibly they will quote the celebrated words, "The Lord is my shepherd, I shall not want." Let us analyze these two over-worked phrases a little more critically. What did the old prophet mean when he said, "seek ye first the kingdom of heaven?" Did he mean to sit around mumbling platitudes? Do men achieve righteousness by merely affirming their desires or striving to psychologize themselves into that state of mind that "God owes them a living?" Is it reasonable to say that the advice of the prophet has been intelligently followed by people whose quest for truth consists of listening to a few talks on divine prosperity? We can scarcely conceive of such to be the case. Rather it would seem that the Biblical advice implies the dedication of the life to a quest of truth and the understanding of those spiritual laws which together constitute the kingdom of heaven. Nor is it at all probable that the reward promised was to be regarded as a material remuneration. He who achieves truth achieves all that is real and truth is its own reward. Truth and real estate are not the same thing nor is that science which is dedicated to the perfection of the human soul to be confused with those arts and crafts which have as their foundation a system of remuneration suitable for the perpetuation of physical society.

As to the opening words of the 23rd Psalm, "The Lord is my shepherd," this is an affirmation of the fact that the human will acknowledges the supremacy of divine will and follows after truth as the sheep follow the shepherd. The 23rd Psalm is not an economic formula, it is a hymn of praise in which a grateful and enlightened soul pays homage to that sovereign truth which supports it through all the emergencies of life. The Psalmist says "the Lord is my shepherd, I shall not want" which is equivalent to saying, "I have given myself to truth—what other thing can I desire?"

To interpret the Scriptures as signifying that a few months study of metaphysics entitles the individual to rest forever on divine bounty is to depart entirely from every sound system of religion, philosophy or sociology that has ever existed.

This letter is a continuation of last month's question. Our problem is concerned with religious and philosophical orientation. Each person brings with him into the present life a considerable background in spiritual experience. We are born the sum of what we have previously accomplished. The ideals and codes of action intrinsic to us bear witness to thousands of years of thought and idealism. To discover where we stand in the spiritual life of the universe it is necessary that we analyze what we believe, for our most secret beliefs and convictions concerning God, nature and life are the true measure of our soul power.

In questing about in life for religious and philosophical systems to inspire and stimulate our present actions we must naturally align ourselves with such modern institutions as are consistent with the spiritual program which we have lived through many lives. It is the natural instinct on the part of man to do this, which results in the perpetuation of numerous sects and cults, all devoted to the same general program but differing in minor details of attitude and method. As growth depends upon an intelligent program, the wise person, discovering in himself that which he needs, next dedicates his thought to the accomplishment of that which is necessary.

Mankind lives and learns along lines of least resistance. In most cases, the line of least resistance is the line of greatest proficiency. We are most familiar with those things which we have most often done. If we have dedicated many lives to the study of a certain philosophy or to the living of a certain code, it is easier for us to continue in that philosophy or code than to branch out into some new or unexplored field of thought or action.

Every human being consciously or unconsciously lives according to the structure of belief built up within his subjective self through the numerous lives that have preceded his present incarnation. Therefore, it follows that if we can analyze correctly what we believe, we shall discover at the same time what we are, and also the quality of the force which motivates our thought and action. We are what we believe. This does not mean that we are greatly influenced by the sectarian attachments of this present incarnation nor are we to confuse names with truth. In each life we call our belief something different, but it is the belief itself and not the name we give to it which must be considered if we are to arrive at the facts concerning our spiritual state.

The psychologist, probing into the subconscious mind for motives and complexes, realizes the significance of those subtle impulses which seem to come from nowhere but are really founded upon ages of assimilated experiences. Every student of the sacred sciences would do well to make a simple psychoanalysis of his own spiritual background. He can take a valuable step in this direction by sitting down quietly and examining his innermost convictions concerning certain great realities of life. Each person who has thought at all on abstract matters has arrived at conclusions, at least to a certain measure, satisfactory and sufficient to his own needs.

Suppose then in connection with this month's letter that you sit down quietly and answer the following questions according to your deepest and most complete convictions. Do not derive your answers from some creed in which you are now interested or with which you have affiliated yourself during this life. Write down the answers that come to you out of your heart of hearts, and then examine the answers critically and impersonally, with the realization that you are examining the summary of many lives of hoping, dreaming and experiencing.

Give your most perfect understanding of:

1. The nature of God.
2. The nature of Nature.
3. The nature of Man.
4. The nature of Soul.
5. The nature of Universal Purpose.
6. The nature of Universal Ultimate.

The way in which each of these is answered will reveal major trends of belief. The great schools of philosophy which have arisen among the empires of antiquity were distinguished from one another principally by the answers which they formulated to these six questions. In many cases, the differences between the schools were more apparent than real. While a few of those most highly proficient in the doctrines sensed the universal concord, the laity of these various religious and philosophical orders were divided by their various opinions even as is true today among the sects of Christendom.

Each of our questions is susceptible of at least three answers and these answers clearly reveal the religious and racial background.

The first question as to the nature of God must naturally be answered from the viewpoint of the patriarchist, the matriarchist or the impersonalist. If we bestow upon God masculine or positive attributes, as is common throughout Christendom and Israel, we are patriarchists. This attitude can be refined until the personal elements very largely disappear and our patriarchy becomes an abstract philosophical concept. We see deity in the aspect of a father, and all creations appear as the children or progeny of this parent. The Romans, Persians, Chinese, some of the Greeks, the Nordic peoples, and the Judeastic cults are the backgrounds of the patriarchist idea.

Among several mystic cults, we have the worship of deity as mother. In the matriarchal system the tender, maternal emotions are bestowed upon divinity instead of the sterner masculine virtues. The father punishes his wayward children, but the mother forgives them and intercedes for them. Matriarchy was at one time dominating the religions of the Egyptians and is generally accepted by many sects of Orientals, especially the Vedantists. With the development of the more sensitive virtues of mankind, female divinities or "Sakti's" become more prominent in religious systems. The matriarchy is a more advanced philosophical concept than a patriarchy to the same degree that compassion and forgiveness are higher impulses than vengeance and retribution.

The third or impersonalistic attitude views deity as principle alone entirely too transcendent to be limited by any concept of polarity. God is defined as mind, consciousness, spirit, truth, virtue, law, or even as in the Socratic philosophies as undefinable, any effort at definition being regarded as a defilement. This attitude is Confucian, Buddhistic, Socratic and esoterically speaking Platonic.

The other five questions are susceptible of similar analysis. Nature was accepted as a god by the Greeks, Hindus and Chinese and as a lifeless and inert vehicle of manifestation by the exoteric Christians and Jews, and as a demon or adversary opposing the laws of spirit by the Gnostics, some sects of the Egyptians and the Zoroastrians.

Man is regarded as a spiritual emanation of divinity itself by the Zoroastrians, Christians and Jews. He is regarded as a personification of the principle of universal intellect or the embodiment of Divine Mind by the philosophers of the classical periods, and as the progeny or child of the earth who must be rescued from inglorious extinction through special dispensations by the Gnostics and several of the religious cults of northern Asia. This attitude also appears among several of the modern Christian cults.

The human soul is derived from the Universal Soul or life of the world by the Platonists and most of the other schools of Greek, philosophy. The soul is confused with God or spirit by the Christians who bestow upon it a certain substantial fabric of its own. The old esoteric doctrines taught that the soul was the experience body of man built up from the accumulated wisdom gained by living. The old Egyptians also concurred with this, for they taught that continuity of consciousness after death resulted in the perfection of the soul body in which the spirit functioned after the decease of its physical form.

The purpose for existence is one of the most important issues of religious disagreement. One school declares the purpose of existence to be the perfection of God; another school the perfection of man; and a third the perfection of the world or nature. The Greeks believed that deity achieved its own perfection through the unfoldment of itself in its progeny. Christendom centralizes all its dogma about the premise that the purpose of existence is the salvation of the human soul. There are a number of groups of the millennial type who look toward to the establishment of heaven upon earth and a Golden Age in which perfection will reign forever in the mundane sphere. Exoterically speaking, the Zoroastrians are representative of this group.

Concerning the question of ultimates. One school acknowledges that at the end of effort there is some final state in which all things exist together in the fulfillment of all hope and aspiration. This may be termed the ultimate doctrine. Then there are the evolutionists who posit growth as eternal and that all natures are unfolding forever and that throughout an immeasurable and limitless eternity there is measureless and limitless unfoldment. This group acknowledges no beginning and no end. Then the third hypothesis is the absorptionist doctrine which has always dominated the highest philosophical systems. This is to the effect that evolution or growth is finally consummated by the reabsorption of all finite life into the infinite Principle from which it had its beginning. This doctrine is particularly prominent in Buddhism where Nirvana represents the return of all individual existence into its Universal Cause. Heaven is the end of the ultimatist, growth is the end of the evolutionist, and Nirvana is the end of the absorptionist.

In addition to these primary questions, there are others which also need to be examined in order to discover the fundamental premises upon which your philosophy of life has been built up. One of the most important of these is the matter of sin. If you refuse to acknowledge the existence of sin through a process of positive denial, you are an absolutionist. If you believe in the forgiveness of sin through divine intercession, you are an atone-ist. If you believe in the unreality of sin, you are probably a Buddhist. If you accept the fundamental existence of sin, you are an anthropomorphist. If you regard sin as synonymous with ignorance to be overcome through the unfoldment of personal integrity, you are then a Platonist and a philosopher.

If you believe in the merit of motive over action, you are an idealist. If you believe that action is the measure of motive, you are a realist. If you believe in the virtue of humility, you are a renunciationist. If you believe in the supremacy of will-power over universal law, you have been imbibing the philosophy of Schopenhauer and Nietzsche. If you believe in the salvation of special classes or types, your background has been among faiths with a strong sacerdotal class or caste as among the Brahmins or Egyptians. If you believe in a god apart from nature, you are a theist or deist.

If you believe that deity is absorbed in its own creation, ruling it from within through attributes and various media, you are a Pantheist. Deism is very strong with the Mohammedans, and Pantheism was universal to the Greeks.

If you believe that perfection is a state of perfect individualism and that you as you will go on forever, to become A god, you are a personalist. If your concept is final identity with and absorption into a greater, all-wise Universal Principle, you are an impersonalist. Most Western philosophy is personalistic, and most Eastern philosophy is impersonalistic. This is really the main point of difference between the two schools.

If you believe in the efficacy of ritualism and hierarchy, you are a ceremonialist and you have come up through religious systems containing pageantry and elaborate priestcrafts. If your attitude towards religion is one of extreme simplicity and you regard all outward religious show as vain, then your background has been among faiths devoted to the teaching of the mystic presence or inner communion and you are an anti-institutionalist.

In your quest for knowledge, if you are satisfied with the understanding of the material world, you are a materialist. If you demand a knowledge of the superphysical causes behind form, you are a transcendentalist. If in transcendentalism, you desire to understand the universal mystery through the rationale of knowing, you are an occultist. If your insight is based upon inspiration and feeling, you are a mystic. If your conversion is influenced by the senses and their reflexes, you are a psychic. The most prominent of the materialistic groups are the rationalists. The most prominent of the occult groups are the Brahmins. The most familiar of the mystical religions is Christianity, and the most prominent of the psychical sects is Spiritualism.

Having examined yourself in an effort to discover the fundamental premises upon which your spiritual life is established, it is then possible to determine with some accuracy that which is logically the next step in your growth and development. This will be the subject of next month's letter.

* * * * *

QUESTION—What place have insects in the scheme of evolution? Are they a legitimate life stream?

ANSWER—In the old teachings, we learn that insect life is the survival of some of the earliest organisms which existed upon the earth. They are stragglers that were unable to keep up with the life waves to which they belonged. They have consequently gone through a certain retrogression and will not be able to continue their unfoldment until the development of a new life wave. They might, therefore, be regarded as minute negative centers of life, exceedingly responsive to the mental impulses of higher organisms. The destructive tendencies in insect life are not really inherent to the insect but are communicated to it by higher organisms. Thus, insect pests, bacterial epidemics, etc. are always aggravated by waves of destructiveness in human behavior. Thus, insects are instruments of Karma and their viciousness is due to the viciousness in human thought and emotional impulses in the animal kingdom. There is an old tradition to the effect that when man achieves to the Golden Age, disease, sin and death will cease and the micro-organisms which now carry disease and torment men will cease their activities. The story of the insect is concealed under the allegory of Pandora and her box.

QUESTION—Why is it that child prodigies in the majority of cases are "burned out" by the time they mature? Why do they not go on developing?

ANSWER—The phenomenon which we call a prodigy in most cases is the result of the unbalance of the endocrine system. The pineal gland controls the flow of mental energy from the ego to the physical brain improper function of this gland may produce the appearance of premature development and maturity. Usually however the physical body is incapable of sustaining the strain of premature activity, and the abnormal condition finally results in the brain or the body breaking down. Children from the fifth to fifteenth year are in the growing periods. During this time, a considerable part of the vital reserve of the body must be expended in building bone, flesh, nerve, and muscle. If during this period glandular unbalance throws a heavy mental or emotional strain upon the body, the vital resources are divided. This results in the final weakening of both the mental and physical processes. Most parents think children are clever if they seem old beyond their years, but the efficiency of the mature individual depends to a great measure upon the normalcy of the childhood and adolescent periods.

QUESTION—Please give your interpretation of the Holy Ghost.

ANSWER—All the great Wisdom Religions of the world agree that the great Causal Energy which we term God manifests throughout creation as a triune or triform energy. Among the Brahmins, the Supreme Deity is represented with three faces and its aspects are designated Brahma the Creator, Vishnu the Preserver, and Shiva the Destroyer. In Greece, the triad consists of Phanes, Chronos and Zeus, and in Christendom, the divine attributes are called the Father, the Son, and the Holy Ghost. These three manifestations represent God as spirit the Bather, God as soul or mind the Son, and God as body or activity the Holy Ghost. In the esoteric system of the Gnostics, the Holy Ghost was the vast active principle which ensouls the material creation. It was termed the Demiurges and is the source of those natural laws by which the economy of physical function is preserved. The Holy Ghost of Christendom corresponds very closely with that which the pagans termed Nature, a term which even now is popularly personified so that we say Mother Nature, regarding Nature as the common parent of all material forms. In Egypt, Mother Nature is represented by Isis who carries in her arms Horus the Christ-child, to signify that soul or mind arises from or is born through the experiences of natural existence. This is the interpretation of the state that Christ, the Messianic soul, is conceived of the Holy Ghost, or arises from the mystery of nature. The word ghost is from gast or a breath. Holy Ghost means sacred breath. This is a symbolical term referring to the breath of life in all things. When the Creative Process formed the world, as described in Genesis, it sent forth Its breath into Its creations and when they received the breath of life, these creatures became living things.

QUESTION—Can peace in the outer life be attained without attaining peace within?

ANSWER—To the average person, peace means happiness. The term actually signifies stillness, and is the dying out of the contentions, frictions and irritations which ignorance and intemperance consistently set up in the human consciousness. There is a wonderful phrase in the Arabian Nights Entertainment: "Happiness must be earned." In these few words is set forth the philosophical formula for well-being. In the same way, peace must be earned. It is the purpose of each evolving soul to perfect within its own nature a condition of wellbeing sufficient to assure tranquility and security. Peace is not in the world—it is in the soul. The contentions of outer existence cease when the soul becomes one with truth. Only when the inner life is established in wisdom can the outer life be at peace with its world.

QUESTION—Do you recommend fasting as a means of advancing spiritually?

ANSWER—According to the opinion of H. G. Wells, Gautama Buddha was one of the three greatest men who have ever lived upon the earth. Buddha's experience in fasting therefore should be of interest and significance to all students of philosophy. When Buddha set forth on his quest for enlightenment, he followed the Brahmin disciple of his time, giving himself over to extreme austerities of the flesh. He performed elaborate fasting's for the purification of his soul until, at last, dying from starvation, he sank down exhausted by the side of the Indian road. His years of self-sacrifice and suffering had failed utterly to bring him the illumination that he sought. Realizing his failure, Buddha ate a hearty meal, and gave up the penitent path of starvation. It was only after he had restored the health and normalcy of his physical body that illumination came to him. It is true that fasting will stimulate the psychical powers by breaking down body resistance, but the way to true wisdom is not through psychism but through the normalizing and perfecting of every part of the nature. In matters of food, the Socratic axiom is admirable: "In all things not too much." Moderation, and not abstinence, is normalcy. The theory of starving to death for the glory of God belongs to the old era of superstitions. The philosopher of today realizes that the law of life is not fulfilled through misery and suffering, but that the universal plan is perfected by the health, happiness and well-being of all creatures.

QUESTION—Does it harm one to attend spiritualistic meetings?

ANSWER—In answering this question, it is not my desire to discredit the sincerity of spiritualists but rather to point out certain hazards which believing people, enthused with an idea, are apt to overlook. A spiritualistic seance is a negative vortex of psychical forces. Such a vortex draws into itself discarnate entities of various kinds and also numerous larvae or elementals of the astral world. The average medium has no power to control the entities which impinge themselves upon the plexus of the sympathetic nervous system. In the séance, both the medium and the sitters are helpless victims of such malefic entities as may care to attack them. Therefore, there is constant danger in seances that the sitters will tape away with them elemental beings which have attached themselves to various parts of the aura. These elementals may later attack the physical resistance by sapping the etheric body. When this condition has gone on for a time and resistance has been greatly lowered, the elemental or malicious discarnate entity may obsess the living person and finally drive the ego out of its body. While such a condition is an extreme case, it is a hazard which every person must be prepared to face who encourages any form of negative psychism or permits themselves to tape part in seances. The miseries caused by the Ouija board, the fallacies of automatic writing, and the general hazard of psychic phenomena has ruined more lives than a few.

QUESTION—What is the proper philosophical attitude towards politics? Should Occult Students tape an active part in political reforms and social programs?

ANSWER—Political science had its origin in the complex of social problems arising in national and racial civilization. Laws are rules of contact and relationship founded upon necessity and intended to sustain individual and collective integrity. As the majority of human beings are neither wholly wise nor wholly honest, grievous evils have arisen. Ambitious men have perverted the interpretations of law to their own profit and, having achieved positions of power and authority, have made other laws for their own advantage at the expense of the public good. There is scarcely a time to be found in history when the political systems of so-called civilized nations were not corrupt. Yet in the face of this general perversion, it still remains evident that laws are necessary, that-government is necessary. The individual must be protected against the schemes of his neighbors and the corruptions within himself. Although most politicians are insincere, political science itself is useful and necessary at this stage in human development. It is natural, therefore, that wise men should desire to correct the evident defects in political systems that mankind may enjoy the protection of honest and efficient codes and statutes. I cannot see how it is possible for a philosopher to ignore the evident need for political reform. At the same time, it is painfully apparent that the wise, being utterly in the minority, can accomplish little by attacking and decrying existing evils.

Nearly all of the great World Teachers realized that the majority of mankind were not sufficiently evolved to solve their vital problem with philosophy alone. The majority benefited most through the correction of the social and economic ills which oppressed them. Buddha bitterly attacked the political theocracy of India, stricking at the very soul of political privilege when he attacked the caste system. Socrates paid with his life for his bitter denunciation of the Athenian policy of privileges and the delinquency of legislators. Confucius devoted his life to the reformation of the philosophies and political institutions of China. Zarathustra first converted the ping to his doctrine that he might begin his reformations with the state. Moses and Aaron defied the Pharaoh of Egypt and Judaism arose on a foundation of social reforms fully equal in significance with the religious purposes. Six of the Seven Sophists of Greece were legislators and political reformists, as were also Pythagoras and Plato. It is generally acknowledged that Jesus was a reformer of Jewish social and political law, and Mohammed fearlessly attacked the whole legislative theory of Arabia, denouncing the privileges of the Meccans and established a doctrine that not only dominates Arabia but encroaches upon every social and political aspect of Islamic life.

It is the duty of the philosopher to labor unselfishly and devotedly for the promulgation of truth and wisdom and justice, and he must perforce withdraw his support from any individual or institution which functions inconsistently with reasonable standards of integrity. On the other hand, political corruptions, like ignorance of which they are a part, cannot actually be remedied by legislation but must be finally corrected by the improvement of human nature itself. Therefore, the philosopher may say—I cannot make a man honest, but if I can dispel ignorance, he will become honest himself. Philosophy always approaches the political problem from an educational viewpoint. If we can make enough people see the reality of those great laws of life which circumscribe all mundane affairs, they will live better as individuals, and the integrity of the individual is the cornerstone of social and political well-being.

QUESTION—What should be the attitude of the Occult Student towards Surgery?

ANSWER—Persons of all beliefs approach surgery with a common dread. The common sense of the individual warns him that the human body is an extremely delicate mechanism which seldom fully recovers from major surgery. The physical man is a masterpiece of natural economy. All the organs and parts of the body have a particular duty to perform and removal of any organ or part is bound to influence the vibratory and chemical balance of the whole structure. Several ancient peoples, most notably the Greeks, held all surgery and dissection in disfavor, declaring it to be a sacrilege against the gods and the human soul to mutilate its house either in life or after death. It is for this reason that the Greeks never achieved any high proficiency in anatomy but did accomplish much in clinical medicine. The clinics of Hippocrates contained hundreds of patients under constant observation but the physicians gathered there possessed only the most rudimentary knowledge of the organs of the body, their location and general structure. Of late years surgery has become more or less of a medical fad and prominent surgeons have grown wealthy off of the exorbitant fees which they charge for even the most minor operations. The average sick person, having little knowledge of his own functions, is intimidated into surgery through high pressure business methods. On the other hand, there are many people living lives of comparative comfort and efficiency who would be dead had not surgery rescued them from some physical extremity.

Philosophically speaking, it seems to me that the matter can be summarized something thus, the purpose of life is experience. Under normal conditions, the perpetuation of life offers opportunity for growth and usefulness. It is the duty of the individual, therefore, to perpetuate life as long as there is any reasonable probability of the restoration of comparative health. To fail in this respect and perhaps to die rather than to use the scientific means available to prolong life would not be regarded as a philosophical virtue, but is technically speaking suicide. Philosophy will permit therefore the use of surgery when other means have failed and surgery is the last recourse. Philosophy would invite each truth seeker to live as nearly as possible in harmony with the laws of health but in an emergency would regard the perpetuation of life as more important than anti-surgical prejudices.

Yours very sincerely,

Manly P. Hall

LOS ANGELES, NOVEMBER 1, 1935

Dear Friend,

To borrow from the terminology of the Neoplatonists, the purpose of mystical philosophy is participation in divine truths. The material universe is the outer court of wisdom's temple. The courses of life were termed by the initiates sacred processionals—the pageantry of being.

Theon of Smyrna, an initiate of the Eleusinian Mysteries, in his celebrated treatise on mathematics, compared philosophy to the rites of the sacred mysteries. He explains that there are five parts to initiation, and likewise five parts to philosophy, through the perfection of which mortals elevate their reason to the "Heroic" state.

Fifteen hundred years have passed since the decadence of the pagan mysteries, but the laws which bound the neophytes of the Eleusinian Mysteries still bind seekers after spiritual knowledge. Theon describes the five steps of self-unfoldment as: purification, TRADITION, INSPECTION, INSTRUCTION and ILLUMINATION. It may be well to explain the use of these terms when applied to the steps of human development.

By drawing upon fragments in the writings of Theon, Empedocles, Plato, Proclus and Olympiodorus, we can prepare an authentic commentary upon the rules of sacred orders.

According to Proclus, the perfective part of philosophy must precede initiation. The perfective part includes two distinct processes. The first is called purgation and signifies the cleansing of the whole nature of its accumulated evil, both bodily and temperamental, for, as Theon says, "the mysteries are not communicated to all who are willing to receive them but only such as possess a purity of life and purpose resulting from certain disciplines of purification." In the sacred school's, morality is the beginning of wisdom and all discipleship begins with self-discipline. The second process involves the positive aspect of integrity. Having cleansed the nature of its terrestrial evils and emancipated it from bondage to appetites and instincts, it is then necessary to perfect within the nature a positive standard of right knowledge and right action. Thus, purification is more than merely emptying a life of its old vices, it is the filling of the life with new virtues and the perfecting of an acceptable standard of personal integrity.

After the processes of the perfective part of philosophy have been achieved, the second step of self-unfoldment confronts the disciple. This is called tradition and is defined in the old writings as becoming acquainted with the sacred fables, legends, myths and rites. We could define it today as intellectual philosophy. The public schools of the present generation teach traditional education, for knowledge passed on from generation to generation is tradition. Tradition is stored in the memory but is not self-motivated. A man may remember all the traditional knowledge of the race and still be unable to think. The memory is only a small part of the mind. Memory stores up tradition but cannot use or vitalize it. Tradition becomes valuable to the individual only when it is vitalized by the reason.

This involves another problem. A child in school who has great difficulty in learning is often referred to as lacking capacity. No individual can be educated beyond his capacity, for there is an inward measure governing all outward things—knowledge with the rest. Traditional knowledge is in itself dead, literal, and often uninspiring. But all tradition locks vital truths within itself. These can be liberated by thought and meditation.

Neophytes preparing to enter the temple of ancient wisdom received the traditions of their order as part of their preparatory rites. Thus, they became aware of the dignity and the import of the institution with which they desired to associate themselves. In addition to a general historical outline, the neophytes received elaborate discourses on cosmogony, the story of the universe, anthropology, the story of man, and psychology, the story of the soul. Disciples finished this period of training in tradition with a reasonably complete knowledge of the laws governing heaven, earth and man. The traditional teachings of the old mysteries are now to be found in the sacred books of the world.

These Scriptures remain locked, however, until memory is vitalized by personal experience.

The third part of initiation is that which is denominated inspection. The neophyte entered the temple at this stage and beheld the initiatory dramas and partook of them. As Plutarch describes in his Isis and Osiris and Apuleius in his metamorphosis, inspection included participation in certain divine mysteries. No complete record has descended among exoteric writings as to the initiatory rituals. The historian Pausanias in his history of Greece, declared that it had been his intention to describe in that work the divine dramas. Even, however, while he was writing the account, one of the gods appeared to him and forbade the recording of the rites. From the brief statement by Apuleius, one fact can be restored. Initiation was consummated by the similitude of death. By their occult arts, the priests induced a trance-like state, suspending all the physical functions of the neophyte. While in this condition the soul of the candidate, released by magical formulas from its house of clay, experienced temporarily the sublime reality of conscious immortality.

As Virgil led Dante through the tortuous passageways of the Inferno, so the Hierophant of the Mysteries led the consciousness of the neophyte through the mysteries of the mundane sphere. This was called inspection because the neophyte viewed as a stranger the universe of wisdom. This same spiritual truth is set forth in the Apocalypse, where the angel or the guide lifts St. John the Seer to the high place and shows him the mysterious City of God.

By inspection, then, Theon inferred the development of those clairvoyant powers by which the sage perceives the workings of the superphysical worlds in the same way that the ordinary person perceives the workings of the material world.

The fourth step is termed instruction. Theon thus describes the end and design of this part of initiation: "And the fourth is the binding of the head and the fixing of crowns; so that the initiated may, by this means, be enabled to communicate to others the sacred rites in which he has been instructed; whether after this he becomes a torchbearer, or an interpreter of the

Mysteries, or sustains some other part of the sacerdotal office." This part of the ancient initiation was also divisible into two processes, the first of which is signified by the "binding of the head and the fixing of the crown." The Hierophant of the Mysteries was regarded as higher than any material ruler and of all men he alone did not bow in the presence of the king. "The fixing of the crown" in the rituals of the Egyptians represented the achievement of mastery and the consummation of the initiatory processes. Coronation has brought the term of candidacy to an end. The stage of adeptship had been reached. Having mastered the lesser thing—himself—the new adept is made master over greater things, becoming a spiritual prince of the universe. "The binding of the head" represents the encircling of the reasoning faculties with a limiting circumference, a symbol of control or direction. The mind is bound to the purpose of the will. The second process of instruction is that by which the new initiate himself becomes a teacher of others, thus paying the debt which he incurred during the periods of his own instruction. In ancient times, only those who had achieved to the fourth degree of wisdom were permitted to be teachers of occult philosophy or founders of sacred schools. Such celebrated initiates as Pythagoras and Plato had successfully passed the grade of instruction before their right to establish communities and colleges was recognized by the philosophical hierarchies. It therefore follows that these great philosophers were trained clairvoyants and had actually explored those mysteries of nature of which they spoke and wrote.

Theon then adds that those who had successfully passed the grade of inspection could become torch-bearers by which he arcanely signified perpetuators of the ancient truths, or interpreters by which he means teachers who might initiate disciples as they had been initiated. Or if they chose, these new initiates might attach themselves to some temple or shrine, holding sacerdotal office as the priests of Delphi who served Apollo, or the Æsculapiads who performed healing through magnetism and occult arts in honor of the god Æsculapius. An initiate of the fourth degree received the credentials by which he might enter the inner sanctuary of Mystery Schools of other nations and peoples than his own. One of the last to receive the fourth rite in the Classical civilization was Apollonius of Tyana who was received with the greatest of dignity by the Brahmin priests of India.

The fifth and last part of initiation is illumination. Of this Theon writes: "But the fifth, which is produced from all these (the four preceding steps) is friendship with divinity, and the enjoyment of that felicity which arises from intimate converse with the gods."

To the initiate the gods were not personalities but states of consciousness—exalted forces moving in space. By intimate converse with the gods the initiate means the elevation of consciousness to a realization of universal and divine reality. Only the highest of the initiates attained to this most exalted consciousness. Nor can any human being at this stage of his development remain permanently in so transcendent a mood. One of the noblest of all philosophers, Plotinus, whose wisdom was second only to Plato's in its sublimity, was permitted on only a few occasions to achieve identity with Universal good. The last words of Plotinus are suitable to one who has gone as far on earth as philosophy can lead a mortal man: "Now I endeavor that my divine part may return to that Divine Nature which flourishes throughout the universe."

The modern application of Theon's outline of initiation may not be at first apparent, but a little thought will reveal its pertinence. The five parts of initiation are the five natural steps in human improvement which follow sequentially when the student has set up within himself a wisely directed effort towards the perfection of his life and being.

The steps of initiation were not arbitrarily decreed by ancient priests. They are levels of consciousness arising from the disciplines of philosophy. The unfoldment of the human soul must conform with certain universal laws inherent to the elements of existence. Growth is progressive obedience. If we would know the secret doctrine, we must set up a certain chemistry within our own natures by the living of the philosophic life. It is because of this fact that we have inherited from the past rules and regulations concerning the conduct and deportment of truth seekers. These rules are "points of entrance" and anyone attempting to come in to the temple by any other way, "the same is a thief and a robber."

Cerberus, the three-headed dog, keeps the gates of the invisible world. Only the one who conquers the three excesses of the animal soul can enter the precincts of the inner life. The Golden Bough of the Mysteries is the symbol of this conquest and is borne by all who set forth upon the great adventure.

The Greeks also symbolized the initiatory procedure under the figure of the Argonautic expedition. The adventures of the fifty heroes led by Jason, like the Odyssey of Homer, arcanely set forth the soul's quest for light. He who would possess the Golden Fleece, the luminous soul-body of the adept, must slay the many-coiled dragon who guards the sacred tree. According to Plato, the blessed theurgist who accomplishes initiation is assimilated to divinity insofar as such assimilation is possible to mankind.

Truth-seekers of the modern world are divided into five grades according to the same order as their prototypes in antiquity. The two lower parts of the sacred order—purification and tradition—are generally termed probationary. The two higher parts—instruction and illumination—are termed culminative or perfected. And the fifth part, which is in the middle dividing the two groups which the ancient's termed inspection, is modernly designated initiation or acceptance into a bona fide school of the Mysteries.

For all practical purposes, average truth-seekers of the modern world belong to the probationary parts of the Great Work. No one seeking enlightenment can achieve his purpose without first satisfying the law through the purification of his life and the enlightenment and perfection of his reason.

It is a great mistake for students of occult philosophy to believe that they can achieve to proficiency in the spiritual sciences without ordering and disciplining thought and action. It is useless for us to regret the disappearance from society of the Mystery Schools of antiquity. Even were these institutions still flourishing in our midst, our present standards of thought and action would deny us any right to participate in their benefits. Not one modern student of metaphysics out of a thousand could hope to be admitted to even the lowest grades of the ancient Mystery Temples.

The real problem that concerns the modern student is not how rapidly he will achieve illumination, but rather how long a time will yet transpire before he puts his foot on the lowest rung of the ladder of preparation. Many students who believe that twenty years of aimless rambling in metaphysics has fitted them for deification must sometime make the sad discovery that there is no haphazard way to truth. It is also sad but true that—to correct an old adage—all roads do not lead to Rome. Only such roads lead to Rome, as actually go in that direction, popular belief notwithstanding.

No disciple of sacred doctrines, no matter how genial or willing or optimistic or generally kindhearted, can expect any result whatsoever from his efforts until he overcomes intemperance and ignorance within himself. Self-discipline is the beginning of philosophy and no one who has not given years to the exact science of self-discipline has any right to claim for himself any distinction in metaphysical matters. It is useless to attempt the development of spiritual faculties while the mind, emotions and the body are without coordination or intelligent and sufficient direction.

All of the great philosophical religions of the world are in complete accord on this point. There is not one exception to this rule. In any nation, among any people, at any time, admission to sacred orders was only possible to those who had first accomplished the mastery of self. It is a sad, yes tragic, state of affairs which confronts the modern truth-seeker. He has been deceived into the erroneous belief that the kingdom of heaven will open its gates to persons who bring no gifts but their own moral and intellectual deformities.

The first duty of those who would be wise is to render temperate all of the intemperance's of the mortal nature. We are creatures of excesses, the tranquility of the soul constantly destroyed by the inconstancies of the attitudes. Philosophy is moderation and all philosophers must be moderate. If we would achieve to truth, we must sacrifice our intemperance's upon the altar of our high resolve. Imminent spiritual achievement is impossible to those millions of human beings whose inner tranquility is constantly shattered by the warring of their notions, opinions and attitudes. As Cicero has so beautifully observed, the wise man is modest in success, patient in adversity, and at peace with all things.

At the present rate of progress, it will be about fifty incarnations before many enthusiastic metaphysicians are at peace with anything, yet this is only the first half of the first step towards enlightenment. A man ascends to the heights of wisdom not upon the broad pinions of enthusiasm but by the slow and arduous course of merit.

Having rescued the nature from the harpies of intemperance, it is next necessary to rescue the soul from that general ignorance which limits all action and denies direction to effort. To overcome ignorance in even the most ordinary matters is by no means an easy task, for man is but a small area of capacity immersed in an infinite expanse of the unknown. Plato recommended mastery in five sciences as reformative. He suggested arithmetic, geometry, stereometry, music and astronomy as good remedies for that stupidity which is a falling sickness of the soul. I fear that such a program will prove discouraging to many people who, knowing little if anything about anything, feel themselves on the verge of cosmic consciousness.

The purpose of the disciplines set forth by Plato is not that man shall accomplish knowledge through them but rather that by the exercising of disciplines man is capable of interpreting the knowledge which is locked within his own spiritual nature. If knowledge is to be released in action, then the vehicle or personality of man must be trained to interpret the light of god within himself. Inward truth can only reveal itself when the outward nature is balanced and informed. The first part of initiation is therefore accomplished when the individual becomes of sound-judgment and in all matters pertaining to material life is well rounded in mental attitude and well-disciplined in emotional and physical action.

Having accomplished this, the disciple is then ready for the second step, or that part which the ancients termed tradition. The modern truth-seeker accomplishes the traditional end of his. instruction best by acquainting himself, through reading and thinking, with the whole theory of philosophical institutions. In an earlier letter of this series, we listed a number of books suitable for such reading. Study follows purification because through the balancing and perfecting of the nature, an inner relaxation is achieved which increases the merit and integrity of mental effort. It will generally take about five years of intelligent and well-planned study to become reasonably well acquainted with the fundamental premises of the ancient Wisdom Teaching. When this course of study is well rounded out and is built into a disposition already refined through consecrated effort, a spiritual chemistry results in the system. The two parts of initiation—purification and instruction—then work together, and out of the combination arises a high degree of inspiration. The student becomes more and more spiritually conscious. It will usually require several lives to exhaust the opportunities of these first two steps in spiritual progress. It is only after this foundation has been thoroughly established and conscientiously perfected that an intelligent truth-seeker permits himself to contemplate initiation into the Great School.

* * * * *

QUESTIONS AND ANSWERS

QUESTION—Is not a physical demonstration of prosperity an evidence that the person has accomplished an inner illumination and is able to control the law of Supply and Demand?

ANSWER—This subject is larger than might first appear, involving several factors which must be considered separately. Persons possessing wealth must derive it from one of three sources: they either inherit it, acquire it through effort, or receive it through circumstances such as the accidents of gift or Providence. In other words, they are born wealthy, achieve wealth, or have wealth thrust upon them. In any case possession is an aspect of karma. If we believe in philosophy, we must acknowledge that no one can possess a great measure of anything except by the decrees of universal compensation. Anyone whose action causes wealth will have wealth or its equivalent in this or a future life. This is only the beginning of the matter, however. Wealth is not an end, but an incident in the unfolding of human consciousness. Furthermore, wealth is one of the heaviest burdens that a man must bear, for by its very nature it is a constant temptation to abuse and misuse. Wealth is not as difficult to achieve as many people believe. Nearly anyone can become wealthy who is willing to sacrifice enough of other qualities to achieve wealth. It is a thousand times easier to be rich than it is to be wise, for shrewdness will accumulate money but only an inner illumination, resulting from hundreds of lives devoted to truth and integrity can result in wisdom, cannot see that wealth is any evidence of spiritual superiority. I would say rather that it is a great opportunity for the accomplishment of good. If this good is accomplished, it is termed in India a virtue, and out of the virtue of many lives comes wisdom and illumination. Soul power is not measured by possession but by the enlightened use of possession. A life devoted to accumulation is not one to pattern after. Wealth, at best, is a material thing beset with material uncertainties and subject to all of the vicissitudes of the physical state. He who possesses it is limited and narrowed by its responsibilities and worries. If wealth descends upon an individual from his karma, it should be accepted with humility and resignation by the spiritually minded person. But to make wealth the goal of living and to spend a lifetime in the accumulation of it can scarcely be regarded as an enlightened course of action. Spirituality infers detachment, or rather, more correctly, an attachment to values. Each person prizes much that which is the measure of his own consciousness. When unfolding reason reveals the beauty and desirability of spiritual things the intellect inevitably turns from low values which no longer satisfy and are therefore no longer proper ends of effort. To say that the demonstration of material prosperity is an evidence of inner enlightenment is to confuse two irreconcilable standards of value. We may as well say that wisdom is worth a dollar and a quarter, or that illumination is worth so much an hour. Spiritual values have no material equivalents, nor are they justified or manifested upon the physical plane. Render unto Caesar the things that are Caesar's but do not try to confuse the law of the spirit with the ambitions of matter.

QUESTION—In what way does an Initiate or Adept differ from an ordinary person?

ANSWER—First we must define our terms. Although the words are often used interchangeably, initiate and adept have different meanings. Technically, an initiate is any person who has been accepted into a body of secret knowledge by some special ritual or ceremony. In ancient times the term initiate signified a man or woman who had passed through the ordeals of the state Mysteries or religio-philosophical institutions of spiritual education. In modern occultism, an initiate is a person who has been accepted into one of the secret schools of natural occultism. In this sense of the word initiation follows years of probationship and preparation. All true initiation is an inner mystical experience and should never be confused with the ritualism of any physical institution, no matter how metaphysical the ritual itself may be in its implications. The word adept signifies one who is proficient in the use of the occult forces of nature, and many years or even lives are required after initiation before this proficiency is acquired. In antiquity, the term adept was reserved for those who had received the Greater Mysteries. They were a small group within the body of the initiates themselves. An adept is one proficient in the most highly advanced sciences of the Mystery School. There are many initiates to one adept. It should be distinctly remembered that both initiates and adepts are human beings, part of our own life wave and differing from ordinary mortals only in the unfoldment of their subjective spiritual nature. The initiate is wiser than the average person, and the adept is wiser than the initiate. But this wisdom should not be regarded as superhuman but rather as a type of enlightened condition towards which the whole race is being moved by the law of evolution. An initiate is subject to the same laws that govern the average man. He is born, he must eat and sleep, and he will pass out of his body in the same way that others do. He is simply equipped to live more constructively and more usefully because he possesses a truer vision of the workings of universal law. The initiate is usually clairvoyant to some degree as this was necessary to his initiation. He may or may not possess the ability to function consciously outside of the physical body. He can read part of the etheric record of the earth and has a considerable understanding of the invisible worlds. He is able to commune with others of a similar degree of development as himself by subjective methods, and he is part of that great Brotherhood of initiates which is being built up in the world as the foundation for the philosophical era that is to come.

All that we have here noted is also true of the adept, but his powers are considerably amplified. He has become part of the mechanism of the great School itself, and unlike the initiate he is not apt to mingle commonly in society but will live apart in some center of the brethren. If he appears among men, it is incognito except to other members of his Order. He is a conscious instrument of the Great Plan and perpetuates his body without the phenomena of birth and death. He does not have disciples other than initiates and it is exceedingly unlikely that he will make his appearance to any person not already highly proficient in occult matters. There is no way in which the average layman can detect an initiate or an adept. But those who have developed a spiritual sensitivity can feel the vibrations of these advanced people. There are also peculiarities in the aura by which they can be detected by those capable of perceiving these superphysical emanations from the body. It should particularly be borne in mind that the state of initiation or adeptship does not release man from the laws governing human life, nor will any adept of the white path ever break natural laws or encourage others to do so. Nor will any initiate or adept use occult power to avoid physical responsibility or pain. It is a law of the Schools that the supernatural powers which man develops must never be used personally or selfishly. It was said of the adept of Galilee: "Others he could help but himself he could not save."

QUESTION—Please tell us something about the antiquity of the Rosicrucian Order.

ANSWER—The Brotherhood of the Rosy Cross is one of the most important occult movements of the Western World, for it most certainly perpetuates the ancient arcana, which is the soul and substance of the Mystery Teachings. Like nearly all metaphysical movements, its history is obscure and where facts are few fables are never wanting.

Modern writers upon the subject of the Rosicrucian's have fallen into extravagant statements concerning the antiquity of the Order. These statements are, for the most part founded upon the highly allegorical account of the antiquity of the Rosicrucian masters published by John Heydon in the last half of the 17th century. History, however, fails to justify Heydon's flights, and his fantastic story can never be accepted as literally true, though, symbolically speaking, it contains much of vital interest.

No bona fide records of the Rosicrucian Society have been discovered that can be dated earlier than the year 1600. In fact, prior to 1610, little of tangible definition has been discovered. The Society itself most certainly came into actual existence about the beginning of the 17th century. Its first publications may have been circulated in manuscripts between 1600 and

1610, but the earliest published evidence of the Order did not appear until 1612 to 1614, when several editions of the fame and confession of the rose cross were in circulation.

It is my opinion, based on considerable examination, that Rosicrucianism, like Christianity, was not a spontaneous revelation but an outgrowth of a chain of adequate causes. Mystical societies in Europe can be traced back through the Dark Ages and finally mingle themselves with the pagan Mysteries of the early centuries of the Christian era. If we speak of Rosicrucianism as a mystical tradition we can trace it back to Egypt and Atlantis, but when we speak of it as a society of men functioning under the laws and regulations of a physical society, organized under the name Rosicrucian, we must then limit ourselves to the opening years of the 17th century.

From about 1610 down to the closing years of the 18th century the history of the Rosicrucian's is rather well established, and we have the names and titles of most of the officers of the Order and an account fairly complete of their rituals and grades and the various reorganizations through which the Society passed. By the beginning of the 19th century, the legitimate history is obscured by so involved a complex of spurious accounts that we may say that the history of the Society vanishes in a general confusion.

Yours very sincerely,

Manly P. Hall

If we admire and venerate those sublime metaphysical teachings which have brought comfort and inspiration to ourselves, we shall accept joyously the meritorious task of disseminating these truths and sharing our inspiration with millions of others whose need is as great as our own.

Among the greatest men who have lived upon this earth are Zoroaster, Confucius, Hermes, Lao Tse, Plotinus, Plato, Pythagoras and Buddha. Individually they brought the light of wisdom into the lives of millions of human beings, and collectively they are the dynamic force behind all civilization and progress.

I believe it is within our power—if we work together—to change the present course of thought in this country and render available and workable those ancient truths which can be the impetus to a new standard of civilization. It is my firm conviction, founded upon a considerable experience, that the most important work to which we can devote ourselves at the present time is the establishment in the modern world of an institution dedicated to the perpetuation and promulgation of that Ageless Wisdom without which no individual or empire can survive.

The influence of such an institution would be two-fold. It will both instruct and inspire. It will instruct through a constant dissemination of ancient knowledge; and it will inspire by standing forth as a proof to all men that the sacred philosophies of the world still live; that sincere men and women are still dedicated to the perpetuation of truth and out of their love and sincerity have erected this physical symbol to their spiritual conviction.

The picture at the top of this page shows the beginning of our building program. On the 18th of October, the work of clearing the land in preparation for the construction of the first unit of the PHILOSOPHICAL RESEARCH SOCIETY was officially started. We need your support in this important and significant undertaking. Gifts or loans in any amount will be gratefully accepted.

Will you serve the future as the past has served you? Noble thinkers have struggled, suffered and died that you might have knowledge. Will you realize that the perpetuation of this Ancient Wisdom is the most glorious work which a human being can accomplish? Let us build a Temple of Truth in a desert of waiting.

Gratefully and faithfully yours,

MANLY P. HALL

LOS ANGELES, CALF. DECEMBER 1, 1935

Dear Friend,

QUESTION—Many metaphysicians claim to have experienced extraordinary psychical phenomena. They describe visions of an amazing nature, asserting that they are able to see and converse with ghosts, spirits, elementals, superhuman creatures, invisible adepts and divinities, and even the persons of the Godhead Itself. Many metaphysical organizations make similar claims, affirming their material movements to be directed by superhuman entities. Please clarify this matter.

ANSWER—The problem set forth in the above question is of the most fundamental importance, yet because of the intimate nature of its inferences it is difficult to drive the facts home to people who really do not want to know the truth. It is very difficult for a novice in things occult to perceive clearly the actual degree to which things super-physical impinge themselves upon our physical concerns. Not only is there a natural ignorance in this matter common to all imperfectly developed mortals, but there is an artificial ignorance caused by the studied dissemination of misinformation on all the phases of the subject.

We all like to believe that our fellow-creatures are honest and sincere, people above ulterior motive and the exploiting instinct, but unfortunately such is not the case. Wherever profit is concerned, man's ethical standards are apt to be corrupted. In all parts of society, the ignorant are exploited by the shrewd, nor has religion escaped the general contamination of the age. Numerous are the lies that are circulated in the name of truth, and equally numerous are the evils committed in the name of good. It seems to be part of Nature's plan that the ignorant must suffer. A wisdom greater than ours has probably ascertained that only through suffering, disillusionment and dilemma can the state of ignorance be made so miserable that mankind will no longer be satisfied to remain therein.

Of those who suffer from the results of their own folly, only a few, however, learn the lessons which experience intends. The majority of people extricate themselves painfully from one evil only to fall into another ill and equally stupid. Yet a man cannot be greater than himself, nor wiser than his own experience. Warnings do little good. Each individual feels himself an exception to the general rule and must learn painfully the moderate course of the wise.

Nearly all religious people have been taught certain reasonable standards of right action, and nearly all religious people promptly forget the practical moralities of their faith. As of the religious world in general, so of the metaphysical in particular. Any person worthy to be termed rational realizes that the universe is bound together by certain laws and principles which cannot be violated and which give to every man according to his works. The numerous disillusionments in metaphysics are due to the failure of common sense and integrity. Under the glamour of the supernatural, the sense of values and proportions is lost and foolishness is rewarded with disaster.

Psychical phenomena is a term to conjure with. Many people feel that it is a special virtue to see things they cannot understand. It is a tragic error to permit occult studies to unseat the reason and destroy the sense of values and proportions so necessary to intelligent living and thinking.

A person leaving an orthodox faith or coming into new thought from the sphere of material science finds the sphere of the occult sciences a world of wonders indeed. To equilibrate oneself in this new concept of the universe is not easy. It is for this reason that the great metaphysical schools of the past permitted only the most advanced types of humanity to become aware of the secret sciences. Since the profaning of the old Mysteries, knowledge suitable only for the wise has become the more or less common property of the unqualified and the uninformed. The result is bound to be philosophical chaos. It is not any longer possible to keep the secret sciences from the profane. It is therefore necessary to instruct the many in the ethics of the divine institution of thought intended only for an enlightened few.

In order to take up the elements of the question, we are going to define our consideration of the whole problem under four headings. There are many aspects to each general issue, but these naturally group themselves into certain classifications. We shall therefore consider the occult factors in modern philosophical thought under the headings:

(1) Deception; (2) Imagination; (3) Hallucination; (4) Illumination.

DECEPTION is our first consideration. The exploitation of the supernatural has been a successful and remunerative profession in human society ever since the beginning of civilization. Religions have been in constant processes of reformation, and reformation is nothing more or less than a revolt against corruption. Wherever deception is profitable, deception must always be suspected. Deception may be profitable either in terms of money or in terms of satisfied vanity. In the case of organizations, the monetary factor is most lively to predominate. In the case of individuals, it is most likely to be the vanity factor.

In occultism, we will use the term deception to cover the general field of religious fraud. The most common variety of this is the procedure of gaining power or authority for an idea by attributing it to some high spiritual source. For example, a man may write a very poor book, the legitimate sale for which would be about 200 copies. But if he suggests in that book or in the publicity attending it that it was dictated to him by a Mahatma, the sale is bound to reach 10,000. It is so easy to say that a Mahatma inspired it. Furthermore, there is no danger of an expose, for no one will ever find the Mahatma in question and the fraud prospers. If anyone should ask where this Mahatma is, the author of the book may glibly reply that it is a secret between himself and the Mahatma and that it is all a spiritual affair which ordinary mortals would not be able to understand.

An imaginary adept also comes in handy in the building of organizations. A half dozen such silent partners mean a large business and a thriving membership. How then is the average person, not conversant with Mahatmas and incapable of recognizing an adept if he saw one, going to protect himself against such deception? There is only one answer—the average person cannot protect himself because he has none of the instruments of reason necessary to unveil the hoax. His good sense may warn him of the deceit but to prove in legal term the fact or misfact of the case is beyond him. The result is spurious organizations are flourishing all over this country, depending for their success upon imaginary adepts or else actually appropriating the names of bona fide initiates without any authority or right to do so. The most outlandish jargon imaginable has been circulated under the presumed authority of the great World Teachers and Messiahs. Indian Mahatmas and Tibetan Lamas are held responsible for pronouncements unworthy of a ten-year-old child. The racket goes merrily on its way, supporting itself by forgery and lies, and deceiving the gullible at a great rate. With such type of movements, all metaphysical implications or claims are deceptions, one of the most profitable deceptions in the world.

Another method of getting authority for a modern notion is to hang it on to some ancient philosophical or religious order. Thus, the Mystery Schools of the classical civilizations are apt to come forth again into this modern generation with nothing in common with their original form but the name. Egyptian, Greeks, Persian, Chinese and European Mystery Schools find their fraudulent counterparts in modern metaphysics. This system, again, is very simple. Supposing that some modern metaphysician with an eye to business decided to restore the mysteries of the Druids. He has a free reign because all of the Druids have been dead for over a thousand years, and there is no one to contradict anything he may care to say. To restore the philosophy of the Druids and their mystery rituals at this time would be an exceedingly difficult matter, but it is not difficult to read a few books on the subject and work out something that contains a little of fact and a vastness of fancy. A few hundred dollars and a little ingenuity, and a modern Druidic Order could be formed which possessed everything relative to the Druids except the true knowledge which they possessed. Documents could be forged, old seals copied, until to the person who knew nothing of the matter, everything would seem exceedingly bona fide. Druidic initiations could then be retailed at a reasonable figure. There could be much high-sounding but non-eventuating philosophy, and thousands of honest, aspiring human souls would be victimized by another deception. If necessary, a couple of old Druid initiates could be produced from the bag of tricks, and they might even sit for their pictures.

The procedure which we have described above has been resorted to time and time again in general outline. But still people who seem to be comparatively intelligent fall under the glamour and believe that at last they have found "the real thing."

Individuals practice deception in occult matters, usually in an effort to appear to be highly advanced or spiritual. A metaphysical form of keeping UP with the Joneses. They read of some unusual phenomenon and immediately report with bated breath that it has just occurred to them. Very often it is a vanity deception which leads later to the founding of spurious movements. A person finds how easy it is to deceive others, and gradually it comes into their mind that it would be profitable to make a business of it. The supposed occult experiences gain for them a new respect and prestige, and they almost invariably finally capitalize this new sphere of influence.

IMAGINATION is our second consideration. Imagination is believing that which one desires to believe, or seeing that which one desires to see. In metaphysics, imaginings are the substance of things hoped for. The mind plays tricks on all of us and the less knowledge use possess, the more easily we deceive ourselves. A trained imagination is a powerful asset and an untrained imagination is an abomination to the reason. Alas, imagination can make adepts of us all!

If it were not for imagination, occult fraud would not be so apt to flourish. Deception and imagination work closely together. One man tells of a psychical experience he never had and immediately somebody else has one just like it. We know of one organization that fabricated a Mahatma out of the whole cloth, and within a few years thousands of students belonging to that organization thought or imagined they had seen or conversed with this Mahatma and were perfectly willing to take oath as to his existence. It is unhappy that weak minds and strong imaginations usually go together.

Imagination is closely involved with reading, listening, studying, and hoping. You all know the story of the man who read detective thrillers late at night, dreamed of the gruesome happenings he had read and woke at two a.m. perfectly convinced that his house was full of murderers and thugs. As soon as he had completely awakened, however, he realized the impossibility of the situation and went back to seep.

But let us transpose this situation a little. Supposing that instead of detective stories the man had been reading fantastic metaphysical literature for several years, without the training or capacity to understand it. After a late evening with his fantastic book, he also had a nightmare. He is in the mood for mystery and when he wakes up at two a.m., he does not realize the absurdity of his dream. His value sense has been undermined by an unwise selection of literature and he is perfectly convinced that he has had an occult experience. He saw gnomes and other elementals, and also, he saw something he thinks was an adept. In the morning he wonders if it was an initiation, and by the next day he is perfectly certain that it was an initiation and that he has become part of the occult aristocracy of the universe. From that time on he always refers to himself and the gods as "we who are enlightened." All a-twitter, this deluded soul reads all hinds of metaphysical literature and haunts occult teachers of several varieties in order to understand his "vision." We have particularly noted how seldom it is that people who claim to see things have the slightest understanding of what they see. After several years of questing, the man who had the nightmare goes into a psychological frame of mind in which he is bound to have more nightmares, and after a few years of this procedure he is ready to start a metaphysical organization of his own. It is a sad but evident fact that many occult movements in the world today have nothing more substantial behind them than a bad dream.

Imagination may afflict in several ways. It frequently gives false reasons to simple and evident things. Ordinarily, when a man stubs his toe, it is an accident, but when a metaphysician stubs his toe, it is either "malicious animal magnetism" or "the black brotherhood." Thus, it seems that imagination also has its morbid side. Everything takes on a supernatural significance. He is the victim of destructive thoughts and he often gets into a situation not so different from the theologians of the Middle Ages who were afraid to go out at night because the devil was hidden under the doorstep. The effect of the constant strain upon the imaginative faculty may also have an unhappy physical reaction. The person becomes tense, nervous and generally upset. The mind becomes a victim of the impulses and a super sensitive psychical condition is often actually produced, which in extreme cases may become psychopathic.

In the last ten or fifteen years, there has been a deluge of outlandish metaphysical writings. They are products of distorted imagination and they will distort the imaginative faculties of weak-minded people who read them. These books have little if any practical value and are responsible for muck occult tale-mongering that brings discredit to the whole subject. All sincere efforts to restore the ancient Wisdom Teachings must battle with the prejudices arising from wild and unbridled imagination. Here again is evidence of what happens when unprepared persons are permitted to play like children with great universal truths. Distortion is inevitable and distortion becomes the foundation of the superstructure of misinformation.

HALLUCINATION is our third consideration. Hallucination may have a chemical origin. It is much more difficult to uproot than superficial imaginings, and often carries with it an authority which leads to extremes of irrationality. Metaphysical hallucinations are similar to mental aberrations arising from the use of alcohol and narcotics. Hallucination is almost inevitable to any person attempting occult study without a well-trained and well-balanced intellect and an emotional nature under good control. We usually think of delirium tremens as a psychical affliction taking the form of violent and horrible experiences which, in advanced stages, is incurable. While this is true of alcoholism and certain other mania-forming drugs, all hallucinations are not of a morbid or terrifying nature, but they all have their origin in a psycho-chemical unbalance.

Hassan Sabbah, the Old Man of Mount Alamut, the founder of the Sect of the Assassins, controlled his fanatical followers by the means of an Oriental drug. This drug produced visions and dreams of ecstatic beauty. The mind floated in a paradisaical sphere. All the evils and worries of life were dissipated. Hassan Sabbah told his followers that this drug gave them a temporary ability to know the bliss of the heavenly state to which they would all go if they died in his service. In the face of this promise death was an experience to be desired and the Assassins gladly exposed themselves to the greatest dangers, inspired by the belief that they would spend all eternity in the heaven of their hashish dreams.

Evangelical revivalism is almost identical with narcotic drugs in its effects upon the psychical organisms of the poorly organized person. By stirring up emotion, an inner excitation is caused which many people believe to be a spiritual experience or an extension of consciousness, but there is a great interval of evolution between an emotional complex and Nirvana. Primitive peoples work themselves into religious frenzies, believing their state of excitement and exhaustion to have something divine about it. Mob psychology and the frenzy of an over-stimulated emotional nature is a physical not a spiritual phenomenon.

Any fanatic is subject to hallucinations because they derange the normal functions of the mind, and there is no fanatic more fanatical than a religious fanatic. Psychical hallucinations arise from an unbalanced emotional attitude toward religion. Such an attitude is most common among metaphysicians and metaphysical movements. No person of intemperate emotions can be in any way certain of the experiences of his inner life. The kind of religious ecstasy of which the average undeveloped person is capable is similar to alcoholism in its hallucinational possibilities. Religion is a serious business for balanced people. Emotionally uncontrolled people will find their way to truth hopelessly obscured by their own emotions.

That there are great initiates and adepts in the world is acknowledged by all of the great systems of esoteric philosophy, but these adepts do not spend their valuable time catering to the emotional sensibilities of silly people, nor are they founding organizations to bestow cosmic consciousness upon foolish mortals who have not yet learned to make reasonable use of human consciousness. What most people call cosmic consciousness is merely a psychochemical crisis in the emotional organism. It may be "full of wonderfulness" but it is no sign whatever of spiritual achievement.

We have examined the "esoteric doctrines" and the most secret inside secrets of several groups of so-called highly evolved metaphysicians who, according to their own statements, spend most of their time communing with adepts. It does not take long to discover that these doctrines are the result either of ignorance or deception. The instructions are either cribbed intact from other works or else are built upon a hodge-podge of borrowed fragments. It is evident to a person of even reasonable mentality that such gallimaufries of error have not descended from great masters of wisdom but are accumulations of metaphysical scraps. The contradictions and confusions given out in the name of wisdom are evidence of childish minds trying to think beyond their own capacities.

Hallucinations may also arise from the result of following false or incomplete methods of "spiritual development." Trick breathing and strange formulae for the unfoldment of the soul are much more apt to lead to hallucination than illumination. No individual can hope to understand correctly any form of knowledge which he has not prepared himself to receive. If spiritual light descends upon a person whose organisms are too low in vibration to receive that light, the result must be hallucination. No one can know more than he is, and anyone who attempts to storm the gates of heaven through organizations or formulae must awake some time to the realization that he is a victim of hallucination. In next month's letter we will take up our fourth consideration, that of Illumination.

* * * * *

QUESTIONS AND ANSWERS

QUESTION—What is the proper philosophical attitude towards suicide?

ANSWER—Several newspapers have recently carried accounts of prominent persons who have committed suicide to escape the prolonged inroads of incurable disease. These accounts have raised the question as to the integrity of such action.

Is a person justified in ending his own physical life if it appears to be no longer possible for him to live a healthy normal and constructive existence?

The attitude of society towards suicide has been subjected to numerous changes and modifications in the thousands of years of social history. Some nations have regarded the action of self-destruction as highly honorable. Others have regarded it as commendable under certain extremities, but for the most part such a course of action has been condemned as irreconcilable with the highest standards of human propriety.

The Mystery Schools of the ancient world were in reasonably complete accord in their condemnation of the deed of suicide. The religio-philosophical institutions taught that self-destruction was an act of violence against the soul. Not that the soul itself could, strictly speaking, be injured, but rather that suicide was a breach of spiritual ethics. Two examples will fairly represent the attitude of the ancients.

In the Bacchic and Eleusinian Mysteries the sacred dramas exhibited in tableau and pageantry the death of the Universal Soul deity Dionysus. This god is torn to pieces by the twelve giants of primordial Chaos who are called the Titans and represent the irrational elements of the material world. After these giants have devoured the body of Dionysus, they are destroyed by the thunderbolt of Zeus who, from their charred remains, formed as from clay the first human beings. The initiates were instructed in the mystical truth that the human body was composed of a mixture of the elementary substances and divine essences, the former derived from the ashes of the Titans and the latter from the blood of Dionysus or Bacchus. Any man who raised his hand in violence against another or against himself was guilty of impiety against the god Dionysus whose essences were mixed with every part of the corporeal fabric. Therefore, the ancient saying, "Who strikes himself strikes the god within him."

Pythagoras held a slightly different view but the substance of his opinion agreed in effect with the older teachings of the original Orphics. According to the Pythagoreans the physical body of man was a living temple within the recesses of which dwelt a divine spirit, one with the eternal nature of God. The body was therefore a temple sacred to divinity, and to defile the body was to defame the "secret master of the house." This doctrine was so literally enforced that none of the Pythagoreans would permit the body to be mutilated either by surgery or autopsy and their opinion so completely dominated Greek culture that medical science was limited to the clinical examination of disease.

The Platonic philosophy somewhat modified the rigid views of the older schools. Suicide was justified in certain extremities, but the whole subject was circumscribed by profound and exact philosophical rules. For example, an initiate was permitted to take his own life if faced by torture intended to force him to reveal the secrets of the Mysteries. He was also permitted to voluntarily sacrifice his life in the service of his god or in an effort to rescue some unfortunate from extreme danger. He was also permitted this extreme action if it was impossible for him to continue in this life on a level of integrity inconsistent with the inner development of his own soul. He might choose death before spiritual dishonor.

In no case however was suicide permitted in order to escape from sickness, sorrow, responsibility, or any material evil which did not afflict the spirit or render the life incapable of further progress.

Corruption is the inevitable end of all flesh, but the deterioration of material fabric does not justify physical destruction while life, opportunity and possibilities of philosophical self-improvement remain. A person who discovers that some disease will permit only a few years or even a few months of life should not think first of self-destruction but rather of the opportunity that yet remains for him to improve in inward knowledge so that he may face the transition with a good hope.

Death is an initiation, into the spiritual mysteries of the inner life, and each man should approach the inevitable end fortified with wisdom and vision. Man begins to die the day that he is born, and, as the poet wrote; "The cradle is ever rocking in the open grave." Therefore, all that man accomplishes in this material sphere he accomplishes while dying. An uninformed man once asked an aged initiate why he did not take life less strenuously in his declining years. The old sage replied: "Life is a race with time and as my course is nearly run should l cease striving or, life the runner at the games, try harder because the goal is nearer?"

The person contemplating suicide would do well to remember the story told of the Greek philosopher who lay dying in the house of a disciple. The friends were gathered in an outer room when a stranger entered with some gossip of the day. Chancing to look through the doorway into the inner apartment where the philosopher lay dying, they beheld him propped up on one elbow listening attentively to the gossip. One called out to him, "Father why do you listen to the gossip of this world when you are so soon to leave it?" "I may be dying" the wise man replied, "but l am not yet dead and while I still live l can still learn."

A wise person does not wreak vengeance upon himself for the evils of his world. He realizes that the purpose of life is the accomplishment of wisdom and experience. Each of the vicissitudes of life brings with it the opportunity to increase knowledge and perfect self. While yet the breath of life is within any body, experience is possible to the soul within that body. Philosophy demands of its disciples that they learn all things well and seek to avoid none of the experiences of this life.

The ancient teachings set forth in symbolic terms the punishments and penalties of suicide. As the great Neoplatonist expressed it, in normal death, the soul separates itself from the body by a natural process. In suicide, the body separates itself from the soul by a violent and irrational action. As this action is contrary to the psychical laws of nature, vibrations are set up which temporarily disrupt the harmony of the soul. For this reason, it is written that the suicide is neither dead nor alive. He has violently destroyed his physical vehicle, but he has not fulfilled the years of his destiny, therefore he must remain in the superphysical elements of the earth to which his superphysical parts are still attached until the normal span of his life, as set forth in the spiritual archetype of his physical existence, has been completed. To such disembodied but not discarnated entities, the ancients gave the name of the "undead." They must continue physical but unseen until the law of their life has been satisfied.

While this circumstance works no permanent hardship upon the soul, which in its natural time is released from this artificial condition, it works a temporary hardship and the suicide discovers that his action has delivered him from no evil, released him from no problem, and preserved him from no disaster.

* * * * *

QUESTION—Does the doctrine of Reincarnation conflict with the teachings of Christianity?

ANSWER—On at least two occasions Jesus acknowledged pre-existence, which is almost equivalent to an actual acknowledgement of Reincarnation. He certainly refers to His Messianic pre-existence in these words: "Before Abraham was, I am." In another place Jesus declares definitely that His Disciples were with Him before the beginning of the world. According to the Gospels, these disciples were ordinary men and there is no inference that they should be considered as divine incarnations or in any way exceptional from other men. To have been with Jesus before the worlds were infers a vast spiritual existence and a continuity of consciousness over a great extent of time. Jesus also inferred that he Himself will return to this world, and this Second Coming, towards which so many pious Christians look, would itself establish Reincarnation beyond debate. The Master further promised that those who believe in His words shall do greater things even than he has done. That St. John accepted the doctrine of Rebirth is evident from the 12th verse of the 3rd chapter of Revelation: "Him that overcometh will I make a pillar in the temple of my God and HE SHALL GO NO MORE OUT. The words "go no more out" are susceptible of no other interpretation than as a reference to periodic returns to an earthly existence for those who have not yet perfected themselves in the mysteries of life.

To sum up the Biblical situation, there is no definite statement concerning Reincarnation in the Bible other than the verse from Revelation just quoted. There are, however, a number of enigmatical statements in which the law of Reincarnation seems to be inferred. Without this doctrine, many of the passages of the Old and New Testaments are meaningless and without point. On the other hand, nowhere in the Jewish or Christian Scriptures is the doctrine of Rebirth assailed, denied, criticized or condemned. The whole subject, therefore, is not a doctrinal issue and the belief in Reincarnation cannot be dismissed as heretical from the words of Jesus or the prophets.

The prevalence of the belief in Reincarnation in the first centuries of the Christian era is evidenced by its wide acceptance by the early Greeks and Latin fathers of the Christian church. It appears also that the Essenes, a religious order of which Jesus is supposed to have been a member, accepted the doctrine of Rebirth, having derived knowledge of it from Pythagoras, the founder of their order. The Gnostics, the most learned of Christian orders, and the first heretics, taught Reincarnation and claimed to have derived their mystical traditions from a disciple of St. Matthew. Reincarnation was defended by many fathers of the early Church, among them Origen, Justin Martyr, Clemens Alexandrinus, Nemesias, Synesius, Hilaria's, and Arnobius. Probably the most outspoken of these Christian patriarchs was Origen, a man who combined a high degree of philosophical insight and true Christian piety. He writes of Reincarnation in this fashion:

"Is it not more in conformity with reason that every soul for certain mysterious reasons (I speak now according to the opinions of Pythagoras, Plato and Empedocles whom Celsus frequently names) is introduced into a body, and introduced according to ITS DESERTS AND FORMER ACTIONS?"

It is generally believed that in the sixth century A.D. the Fifth General Council of Constantinople anathematized Reincarnation, but it is now evident that this prevailing prejudice is unfounded. To quote the Rev. A. Henderson, Vicar of St. John de Sepulcher, Norwich:

"A further objection which exists in the minds of many is based on the supposed condemnation of the doctrine by the Church in the Fifth General Council of Constantinople. A careful consideration of the historical situation makes it abundantly clear that the question of Reincarnation was not even raised at the Council; and that the condemnation of certain extreme tenets of the Origenists was the act of Mennas, Patriarch of Constantinople, in the Provincial Synod. In this he was instigated by the Emperor Justinian, who ordered him to procure the subscription of the bishops to the anathemas. This local synod was held in A. D. 43, while the General Council did not meet until ten years later. It is easy to understand, however, how this extra-conciliar sentence of Mennas was, at a later period, mistaken for a decree of the General Council."

The above quotation clarifies two points of controversy; first, the problem of Reincarnation was not even considered by the Fifth General Council; second the Provincial Synod directed against the Origenists makes no specific reference to Reincarnation and there is no way of proving that the doctrine of Rebirth was even one of the "extreme tenets" which had irritated Justinian. It therefore follows, as Mr. G. R. S. Mead, an eminent scholar in matters of early Christian tradition, has observed, that the Christian Church has never formally anathematized Reincarnation.

E. D. Walker, in his valuable work, reincarnation includes the illustrious name of St. Buenaventura among the many churchmen who favored the doctrine. Prof. Wincenty Lutoslawski, in his important book pre-existence and reincarnation, writes thus of Rebirth:

"It finds favor even with Roman Catholic theologians, amongst whom was the great scholar, Monsignor Archbishop Passavalli (1820-1897) who not only declared that Reincarnation is not in conflict with Catholic dogma, but himself accepted the doctrine, at the age of sixty-two, from two disciples of the Polish School of Philosophy, and lived up to the age of seventy-two, unshaken in his conviction that he had lived many times on earth and that he was likely to return!"

The attitude of the Christian Church in the twentieth century on the vital issue of Reincarnation is best summarized in the opinions of two leading churchmen. Cardinal Mercier, the heroic Prelate of the Belgians, representing the opinions of the Roman Catholic faith, while not committing himself to a personal belief in Reincarnation, has definitely stated that the doctrine is not in conflict with Catholic dogma. For Protestant Christianity, Dean Inge, late of St. Paul's London, assumes a similar attitude, finding no conflict between this "the oldest creed" and modern Episcopaleanism.

From the preceding, there is reasonable assurance that the modern Christian can incorporate the doctrine of Reincarnation as a part of his religious belief and remain safe within "the odor of sanctity."

Sincerely yours,
MANLY P. HALL

LOS ANGELES, CALF. JANUARY 1, 1936

Dear Friend,

This month's letter is devoted to the problem of illumination, as understood in its mystical sense. The term illumination was first used by the early Christians to signify baptism by the spirit. In the Middle Ages, a sect called the Illuminati sprang up, and it is from the traditions of this order that the Illuminist doctrines of today have their origin. The principal doctrine of illuminism is that man can be wholly possessed by the light of truth. We may, therefore, create a metaphysical definition for illumination in the terms of mystical Christianity. When the grace of universal truth comes to any man and abides with him, that man is illumined.

It might seem from such a definition that the whole problem is a simple one, but unfortunately a number of extremely difficult factors present themselves. In the first place, illumination is a word representing a very abstract idea. Although the rides of language have been pretty well fixed in the last two hundred years, the meanings of obscure words or those pertaining to spiritual mysteries are still comparatively uncertain. We use words to communicate ideas but while the ideas of men are modified by innumerable shades of meaning, language, which is comparatively inflexible, is seldom a complete or adequate vehicle for the complete communication of thought. For this reason, even carefully chosen words often convey an inadequate or even false impression. Especially is this true of the English tongue which has developed an amazing industrial vocabulary but is weak indeed in transcendental terminology.

An even more disastrous equation is the weakness of man's interpretative power and his comparative ignorance of the actual meanings of the words and terms of his own language. The average vocabulary is only six hundred words, of which most are of one or two syllables. Even these words are loosely used and inadequately interpreted. When difficult or obscure terms are used in speaking or writing, the average person must guess at their meanings and arrive at certain generalities by context, while fine points elude the uninformed until the values of meanings are hopelessly obscured.

The word illumination is peculiarly difficult. First, because of its fundamental inadequacy to state in which it is used to define; and second, because its metaphysical inference is entirely beyond the experience of those using the term. In modern metaphysics, the word illumination is applied to the whole gamut of subjective reflexes from ecstasy to hysteria. Before we can hope to make any useful contribution to the literature bearing on the subject of illumination, we must rescue the word itself from the present confusion of tongues and establish it as signifying a certain particular and specific state of human consciousness.

All rational men desire truth. The quest for enlightenment is co-eternal with the instinct to live. The nobler impulses may be temporarily obscured by the material instincts but the nobler part of life finally reasserts itself, impelling humanity to essential progress. In this search for enlightenment, man has formulated two major concepts of the nature and substance of truth. These we will now examine.

The ancient world postulated a universal consciousness distributed throughout creation, supporting and sustaining all things by virtue of its intrinsic perfection. The universe and all that it contains was produced by Absolute Truth, is maintained by Absolute Truth and is moved inevitably towards ends determined before the processes of creation had brought forth the world.

The modern concept is very different. The universe is regarded as alive but not conscious. Knowledge is looked upon as accumulative and to man is assigned the task, of revealing truth by an infinite labor through incalculable periods of time. In other words, there is no knowledge until the mind discovers it, and to the modest scientist, science itself is the regulator of minds and the custodian of all knowledge. It is inevitable that two such conflicting viewpoints would build about themselves equally divergent schools of thought. Philosophy, the mediator between all the extremes in nature, acknowledges a certain integrity in both viewpoints and combines both postulates in its program of human enlightenment.

Our modern civilization is keyed to the scientific notion that all knowledge arises from the desperate struggle of the mind to gather and reconcile the vast body of data which has accumulated through the centuries and now forms the body of learning. Education, therefore, consists of filling modern minds with the opinions of the ages. This same viewpoint has also come to largely dominate religion. Religious training consists largely of listening and agreeing. This explains why so little vitality remains in the theological systems of our day.

Various schools of mystical philosophy have formulated their own definitions or equivalents for the term illumination. To some, the word signifies a complete absorption of the self into the impersonal essence of universal life. To others the term implies awakening of the subjective self and its complete absorption of the individuality and purpose of the objective nature. If illumination has any meaning at all to us, it must signify an extension of all the rational virtues of the mind and soul. Enlightenment is superiority, not the assumed grandiloquence of the proverbial Hornblower but an essential greatness marked by an appropriate modesty of attitude and action. Illumination is not bestowed, it is achieved.

There is no more ridiculous pretense in the whole sphere of pseudo-occultism than the promise of illumination held out to stupid people as a bait to swell the ranks of some worthless metaphysical cult. In the last fifteen years I have come across a considerable number of pseudo-illuminated metaphysical Pharisees suffering from one of the most objectionable forms of the superiority complex. As their problem is a common one, constantly recurring from year to year, it may be generally useful to examine it critically.

Having examined the pretenses of a number of persons of different cult affiliations who claim to enjoy a specific form of illumination, I find that their claims to special enlightenment may be, for the most part, classified under a few simple headings. Of course, occasionally an entirely new type of fraud comes along, but for the most part the shysters run true to form—seeming to lack originality along with the other virtues. To classify the exhibits:

1. An emotional person who takes "advanced," lessons from some occult teacher who claims to be a master, enjoys a neuro-psychic thrill at the thought of being so close to a "mahatma" and mistakes these "jitters" for a high degree of spiritual vibration. Romantic inhibitions and hero-worship are also factors in this form of illumination.

2. At the present time there is an exceptionally choice assortment of cults and groups claiming to be the "one and only inspired source of perfect wisdom and complete understanding." It naturally follows that when some benighted mortal falls under the influence of such absurd pretenses, he is almost certain to feel that he participates in a high and exclusive consciousness. The pleasant sense of these feelings often passes off as illumination.

3. Then there is the special formula illuminate. He is the type who has paid over well for some metaphysical catch phrases and formulas which he uses as aids when going into the silence or as a means of producing

auto-hypnosis. Such a person may have a few mild psychic experiences, or think that he has, so he rests upon his laurels and discusses illumination in a personal and authoritative sort of way.

4. Then, of course, there is the initiate-illuminate who has taken sixteen degrees in some utterly worthless secret society and is completely intoxicated by the realization of his own importance. He also has access to "esoteric documents" which have nothing of any importance in them and feels with all due modesty that he is entitled to regard himself as "almost" an adept. This type is often found sitting around waiting for cosmic consciousness, with the firm conviction that it will arrive at any moment.

5. The next type is the mis-information illuminate. His consciousness is completely overwhelmed by the "cosmic truths" which have been imparted to him by some metaphysical scallywag. He will tell you in the most awed sotto voce that only his prayers are preventing the next world war, or that if it were not for him and other contrite souls California would slip into the Pacific Ocean. He may also pass on to the privileged few the important spiritual fact that archangels always part their hair in the center.

6. Then, last but not least, there is the most stubborn and irrational of all the pseudo-illuminates —the personal experience illuminate. He sees things and has experiences, initiations and soul flights. Having no knowledge whatsoever of occult matters, he is one of those poor souls who gets mediumship confused with mastery and writes books on cosmic consciousness.

Of course, there are modifications and sub-varieties but these are the most common and most typical and account for nearly all of our so-called illuminates. The fact of the matter is that the average student of metaphysics has no concept whatsoever as to the nature of illumination and is therefore in no position to protect himself against foolishness and chicanery.

It seems to me that one of the main causes of metaphysical misunderstandings is the time equation in personal development. While it is true that time itself has no spiritual existence, it is also true that while we live in the material world, our activities are measured and circumscribed by the time factor. Impatience is an unphilosophic attitude, and in the task of perfecting oneself, there is no successful way of hastening natural processes beyond a certain systematic endeavor. We should stop thinking of perfection as something just around the corner and admit the evident fact that at the present rate of progress, it will be many lives before anything resembling perfection can be reasonably expected. To extend his spiritual powers, a person must be prepared to devote an appropriate amount of time to his endeavors.

Take, for example, the average metaphysician. Up to middle life, there was probably little, if any, interest in philosophy and self-discipline. At about forty metaphysics was contacted. For the next ten years there was some reading, possibly attendance of lectures on assorted subjects by strangely assorted teachers. These ten years also brought many disillusionments and the total progress for the period could not be regarded as very intensive or consistent. But ten years seems a long time to the person totally unacquainted with cosmic immensities, and the mind begins to entertain thoughts of illumination, rewards and universal beneficence. These rewards, being totally out of proportion to the merit of action, do not manifest themselves and impatience grows where patience itself was never cultivated.

Once upon a time, I met a dear old soul who for all practical purposes epitomizes an entire class of human beings. She had been in "new thought" for nineteen years, a period which to her mind was just a little short of infinity. She could not conceive that there could be any more to know, or any further accomplishment possible. She could quote fluently the platitudes of prominent metaphysicians, she had read all the books, attended all the lectures, and knew all the answers. Perfectly sincere, as far as stupidity can be sincere, she was settling back to await the downpouring of cosmic consciousness. She fully believed she had earned illumination, and its failure to appear was a distinct miscarriage of divine justice.

The facts this kindly person did not realize are that art is long and that the human mind has not yet been formed that can possess all in itself. Illumination is not a matter of nineteen years or nine million years. It is a matter of the unfoldment of the inward self. It may require a thousand lives to release the soul powers from the entangling corruption of matter. Only a very few human beings have labored so intensely and achieved so fully in their previous lives that they can reasonably expect even a moderate degree of spiritual awareness in this present incarnation. Instead of worrying about cosmic consciousness, which after all is only a term signifying a spiritual state far beyond present probability, rather dedicate the present life to a program of intelligent and reasonable progress. It is not that we should die perfect but rather that we should die better than we were born. All real growth is gradual, gentle and sure. It is natural that we should all aspire to a divine estate, but reason dictates an intelligent preparation and a consistent program of action.

Our term illumination has much in common with the Buddhist term Nirvana, or the Absolute of Absolutism, or the cosmic consciousness of New Thought. No human being can accomplish these final ultimates and still remain a human being in contact with other mortals of this world. Individuality retires gradually towards infinities and is finally absorbed. The term illumination, however, has a slightly different inference in practice, from finalities; for example, illumination is progressive. It is a constant, endless unfoldment.

I would like to establish a series of definitions and explanations which I hope every student of occultism will understand and make a part of his philosophy of life:

1. Illumination is man's conscious entry into the sphere of spiritual understanding. It is, so to speak, the soul's coming of age. In the physical life of man, it corresponds to maturity. It is the condition of having outgrown the material illusions which dominate the infancy and childhood of life. As it is impossible for the child to gain the experiences of life except by growing through its several ages, so it is impossible for consciousness to be released into maturity of expression without passing gradually through the educative disciplines imposed upon it by natural law.

2. Illumination can come only to those who have merited it by many lives lived in absolute dedication to the cause of truth. Illumination is not primarily dominated by the factors of this present incarnation. It belongs to the great life cycle of the spirit and not to the small cycle of personality of which the present birth and death are the boundaries. Illumination is the most important spiritual fact in our cycle of existence, but it does not necessarily occur in this life or the next. It occurs when merit determines.

3. Illumination is only possible to those who have already highly refined and perfected every aspect of life and action. This refinement, the result of many lives, is revealed in the temperance of the nature in the present life. Uncontrolled emotions, destructive actions and perverse thoughts cannot exist in a highly evolved person. No individual who is incapable of controlling his own destructive tendencies can hope for any form of illumination until these evil tendencies have been mastered.

4. Illumination is an intensely internal experience arising from the chemistry of merit. Like initiation, illumination is an alchemical mystery. It is part of the Rosicrucian mystery of the transmutation of metals. It is called

tincturing. It is the light of the soul shining outward through the body and transmuting every particle of the material nature with the power of beauty, virtue and wisdom.

5. Illumination can come only to the most highly advanced types of human beings. It is not to be found among inferior types because they are incapable of releasing spiritual powers through poorly organized bodies. Such illuminated human beings as Pythagoras and Plato possessed highly refined organisms, the result of many incarnations devoted to sublimating material principles. Such refinement of organism is absolutely indispensable to any high degree of spiritual progress.

6. Illumination never comes to a person incapable of understanding it or appreciating its significance. It is not unusual for people to go to a teacher of the occult sciences to have their psychic experiences diagnosed and interpreted. One will say, "such-and-such a thing happened to me—was it initiation?" Another will say, "I saw some funny lights last night—am I illuminated?" It is a rule that all can depend upon that no one will be illuminated or initiated without knowing it. The reason is very evident—no one can be initiated until he has reached a state of development in which he is perfectly qualified to decide for himself the significance of his mystical experiences. A person who does not know whether he is illuminated or not very evidently is not, for illumination itself could scarcely fail to clarify this problem for him.

7. Illumination is never bestowed upon groups or orders nor at any specified time or place by rituals, formulas, lessons or esoteric revelations. One of the reasons why it is never bestowed upon groups is because there is no recorded incident where a number of people ever merited it at the same time or under the same conditions. In fact, but one or two persons in a generation achieve it. All pretenses to the effect that illumination is communicable are in themselves fraudulent, for not only is it an individual experience, but there is no language known to man by which the consciousness of illumination could be transmitted from one to another.

8. Illumination, or anything like it, can never be promised by anyone. No person who would promise that he could bestow illumination is worthy to possess it and any person expecting another to illuminate him shows by his own ignorance that he is unworthy to receive such a boon. In all the ancient Wisdom Teachings disciplines prepare disciples for spiritual awakening but the awakening itself is a divine chemistry entirely beyond human control and regulated by the law of Karma.

9. Illumination is not a substitute for virtue, effort or discipline, but rather it is the reward for high accomplishment in all these virtues. These kindly folk who believe that spiritual realization will relieve them of all their earthly responsibilities have too much of theology and not enough of philosophy in their souls. Theology teaches man to cast his burdens on others but philosophy to carry them himself. Illumination is not the beginning of occultism, but the end of it. Few seek wisdom for its own sake, the most desire it only as a solution to the discomforts of life. While wisdom certainly releases man from bondage to trivial annoyances, it also bestows upon him a larger responsibility than he ever knew.

10. Illumination does not cleanse men of the evils of their own natures, but rather comes only to those who have already cleansed themselves by the disciplines of philosophy. There are thousands of metaphysicians who believe that when they get the mystic formula of peace, power and plenty, all their evil disposition will be cleansed in the twinkling of an eye. The truth of the matter is that their spiritual extensions of consciousness will never arrive until the life itself has been put in order. As the old philosophers have told us, if we desire the spirit of God to come and dwell with us, we must cleanse the temple of all unworthiness and rededicate it to the principles of truth and justice.

* * * * *

QUESTIONS AND ANSWERS

QUESTION—To what degree is a university education useful to a person interested in the perfecting of his inner spiritual life?

ANSWER—The answer to this question must be understood to be an entirely individual matter. To some higher educational opportunity is of the greatest importance, whereas to others it is comparatively meaningless. Education does not ensure spiritual superiority, that is the type of education to be secured from our colleges. On the other hand, education can bestow capacity and appreciation, and, all other things being equal, may be an aid to the appreciation of metaphysical values. The ancients regarded education as a prerequisite to philosophy. Pythagoras would accept no disciples who had not achieved scholastic honors; and Plato caused a panel to be placed over the gate of his school on which were the words: "Let no man ignorant of geometry enter here." The value of so-called higher education depends upon the motive which moves the student to learning and also the mental capacity of the student himself. Of course, youth is without the experience necessary for the higher appreciation of educational opportunity, and very few college students are moved to their studies by any great spiritual aspiration. It is only years afterwards when most of the schooling has been forgotten that the mature person begins to wish that he had been more attentive in his periods of learning.

One of the greatest students of comparative religion and philosophy in the modern world was deprived by poverty of the benefits of a university education. General Albert Pike, soldier, scholar, philosopher and Freemason, was turned from the house of learning because he could not pay the matriculation fee. Thus denied, he educated himself and became one of the greatest scholars of the modern world. In his advancing years, the university which had refused him admission offered General Pike an honorary degree. Pike declined, saying that when he had needed the university it had refused him and that he now had no use for its honors. After his sixtieth year General Pike mastered the Hebrew language, also the Persian tongue, and Sanskrit, and translated the sacred scriptures of the Jews, Persians and Hindus, with numerous important commentaries.

Education is necessary to philosophy but education is not always to be secured from those institutions presumably dedicated to its promulgation. The shallowness of our present educational theory means usually dubious returns for the years spent in the modern college.

QUESTION—Do you believe that we are about to enter the Golden Age?

ANSWER—In the mythology of the Greeks, the life of the earth is divided into four great periods, called Ages. The first was the Golden Age, the second the Age of Silver, the third the Bronze Age, and the fourth the Age of Iron. These ages correspond with the Yugas of the Hindus, which also divide the cycles of evolution into quaternary periods. The Golden Age of the Greeks is described by the poets as a time in which no evil existed, and all nature dwelt together in beauty and harmony. Neither sin nor death had come into the world and Pandora's box with all its ills had never been opened to lose its misfortunes upon man. For thousands of years, the idealists of the race have dreamed of the return of the Golden Age. They have envisioned man growing wiser and less selfish, evil ceasing and humanity restored at last to an enlightened and cooperative condition.

There is no evidence, however, at the present time that we are in any imminent danger of a general reform. Men grow more selfish with each passing day and we must experience much more of sorrow and suffering before we will voluntarily dedicate ourselves to a program of enlightenment. We now live in the Age of Iron or the Kali-yuga or Black Age of the Hindus. Until this cycle ends, and alas many thousands of years remain yet to run, we cannot look for the return of the Paradisaical state described in the ancient fables. Yet the Golden Age must finally come again, for all the progress of the race—though slow and apparently uncertain—is leading inevitably to a better day when humanity, tired of self-inflicted woes, will depart from their present course of evil and bring to reality the Utopias of their dreams.

QUESTION—What is the Trinity?

ANSWER—Nearly all of the great religious systems of the world represent their supreme Deity as manifesting through a Trinity or triad of attributes. The origin of the doctrine of the trinity is too remote to permit of discovery and analysis; but the belief that universal energy manifests triadically appears to be justified by the findings of modern science. Deity was frequently symbolized by the ancients as an equilateral triangle. Pythagoras represented divinity under the form of a triangle of dots to signify the divine power and its extensions or manifestations. In India, the trinity consists of the creative, preservative, and disintegrative aspects of universal life. These powers are represented by three human faces united in one head, as in the Trimurti of Elephanta, this composite figure representing the triple mystery of the Godhead. In Christianity, the Father, Son and Holy Ghost are the three persons of the Trinity or triform-unity. The three divine powers emanate from themselves the three worlds or planes of existence, termed heaven, earth and hell in Christian theology, or in the terms of Platonic philosophy the spiritual, intellectual and material creation. In the old Mysteries, the three powers of the creative triad are called will, wisdom and action, or consciousness, intelligence and force. These powers are sometimes represented as three pillars or columns, as in the case of the Kabbalah. These pillars are referred to as the triple foundation of the world and represent the three forms of universal energy by which the equilibrium of creation is preserved.

QUESTION—Have we entered the Aquarian Age yet?

ANSWER—There is some difficulty in determining astronomically the actual time of the Suns ingress into a zodiacal sign. Certain arbitrary factors must be accepted before any satisfactory calculation is possible. According to the opinions of modern astronomers the Sun is now in about the 8th degree of Pisces, and therefore has about 8 degrees yet to retire before it retrogrades by the processional motion out of the sign and into Aquarius.

The processional motion is about 1 degree in 72 years. According to this calculation it will be nearly 600 years before the Sun actually enters the sign of Aquarius at the Equinox and the Aquarian Age has its beginning. Of course, the Sun changes degree every 72 years and these degree changes are in themselves capable of producing a considerable change in the life of man. I know that several metaphysical movements are of the opinion that we have already entered the Aquarian Age or will very soon do so, but I do not believe that these organizations can justify their opinions astronomically.

QUESTION—Some time ago I went to an Evangelistic meeting and during the service there were people who took the baptism of the Holy Spirit. They became hysterical and rolled on the floor for over an hour. They were supposed to be under the power of God. I would like to know your opinion regarding this?

ANSWER—Religious hysteria plays an important part in many of the world's theological systems. Prom the Shamanism of primitive cults to such elaborate religious institutions as Christianity, hysteria is an important equation in the phenomenon of faith. Most people of devout religious leaning are intensely emotional. Orthodox theology is for the most part a faith of inhibitions. For many hundreds of years, it was regarded as a theological sin to be comfortable, and to be happy endangered the immortality of the soul. A creed which constantly preached "thou shalt not" and constantly limited the normal emotional expression of its followers was certain to bring a goodly number of its parishioners to a state of psycho-emotional hysteria. Imagination stimulating emotion must result in emotional crisis. Of course, people rolling on the floor are not filled with the Holy Spirit, nor are they under the power of God. They are simply in an emotional spasm and have lost all semblance of self-control. These spasms are very detrimental to the bodily harmony, and a person who too frequently gives way to them will destroy emotional poise and mental balance. It is incredible that in this enlightened century the most primitive and barbaric forms of religious sorcery should still be widely practiced under the name of Christianity.

QUESTION—What is the Philosopher's Stone?

ANSWER—The alchemists of the Middle Ages, following the ancient formulas of Hermes the Egyptian, sought to accomplish the three ends of the Hermetic Art. The three goals of alchemical research were the Elixir of Life, the Philosopher's Stone, and the transmutation of metals. The Elixir of Life was the mysterious subtle essence which healed all disease and bestowed immortality. The Philosopher's Stone was the mysterious ruby-diamond or the blood-diamond, the Wise Man's Stone, which bestowed all knowledge and power and rulership over all the forces of nature. The transmutation of metals was the secret of regeneration, the restoration of all the corrupted values of life, and security. Of course, alchemy was divine chemistry, the secret of the perfection of life through the disciplines of wisdom. The Philosopher's Stone was the perfected inner life of the individual, his own diamond soul. He who perfects his own soul possesses the touchstone of the wise. The luminous soul-aura of the enlightened human being is the symbolical diamond, and he who has achieved to it lacks nothing that is necessary to wisdom and divine authority. The laboratory is life, the retort is the body of the alchemist himself, and the mysterious processes which tape place within the retort represent the transmutation of the base elements of life, brought about by the living of the divine art.

QUESTION—Please tell me what books will assist me in the study of the Sacred Magic of the Kabbalah, numbers, etc., and where I can obtain them?

ANSWER—The Kabbalah has been called the Secret Doctrine of Israel, and is one of the most important sources of the Ancient Wisdom Teachings. Eliphas Levi, the French Kabbalist, wrote that the three most important books of the Kabbalah are the Zohar, the Sepher Yetzirah, and the apocalypse. The Zohar has been recently translated into English for the first time and is published by the Soncino Press, 5 Gower St., London, W. C. The Sepher Yetzirah can be ordered from any bookstore dealing in second hand occult books. Several editions exist in English. In addition to these works, there are several authors who have written explaining or interpreting Kabbalistic though. Isaac Myer, Arthur Edward Waite, Franck, Ginsberg and MacGregor Mathers have all written readable works on the subject. The great textbook of Kabbalism is the kabbala denudata published in 1677 in Latin only by Knorr von Rosenroth. This book may be consulted in the San Francisco public library, the New York City Public library, and in the Library of Congress.

Books dealing with the numerology of the Kabbalah are extremely scarce. The only works 1 have on the subject are in manuscript. Authentic books on any phase of numerology are extremely rare and the popular available writings are of doubtful importance. Stanley's history of philosophy has a good article on the Pythagorean theory of numbers. Thomas Taylor's theoretic arithmetic is the most important textbook available on this subject.

Wynn Westcott's numbers is a small but interesting handbook. I hope at some future time to be able to publish some of the old manuscripts on numerology in our collection.

Sincerely yours,

Manly P. Hall

MAY THE NEW YEAR BRING YOU ENLIGHTENMENT AND PEACE

LOS ANGELES, FEBRUARY 1, 1936

Dear Friend,

QUESTION—If it is the purpose of the Occult Sciences to perfect the individual in the philosophic virtues, why are so many people interested in Metaphysical Subjects so ladling in the rudiments of discrimination and poise?

ANSWER—No branch of learning can flourish in an atmosphere of inadequate scholarship... The popular mind is not erudite. This is particularly true of the metaphysical mind in America today. The present generation is not distinguished by any high development of acumen. Education is regarded as a sort of drudgery, a necessary evil, by the majority. Nearly all of the standards of knowledge have been compromised, with the result that superficiality is the keynote of the hour. Broadmindedness is a virtue if the mind possesses the capacity to be broad. It is not broadminded however to be merely scattered. It is virtuous to acknowledge the probability of the presence of good in all things but it is beyond the capacity of even the wisest to attempt to practice "the good in all things."

The last thirty years have greatly altered the standards of living and thinking. The cultural standards of the last century have passed away. Simplicity has given place to complexity in every department of living. Life becomes increasingly difficult with each passing year. The capacities of the individual are challenged. Each person must live a larger, fuller life if he is to survive.

The changes that have been wrought in the present century do not necessarily reflect the status of the majority of humankind. Our present involved and fast-moving tempo arose from the genius and ingenuity of less than a hundred men whose inventions and discoveries changed the whole course of life of some two billion of their fellow-creatures. The majority became the heirs of the minority, but it cannot be truthfully said that the majority sensed or understood the momentous consequences of the changes taking place.

Most people are living in a world entirely too vast and too involved to be intelligently analyzed. It is a dangerous thing to live in a system that we cannot live up to, but of course, it is impossible to live up to a social pattern beyond the capacity of the intellect. Superstitions always arise from the failure of understanding. It is evident to all serious thinkers that the present generation is superstition-ridden. You will remember that on one occasion, Lord Bacon affirmed that unbelief is the grossest superstition of all. The rapid development along industrial and economic lines has focused man's attention almost entirely upon material problems. The result has been a general collapse of the spiritual standards of the race. It is true that man must always worship something, but he no longer feels the need of venerating the gods abiding beyond the firmament.

Fascinated by his own ingenuity man turns his veneration upon his own handiwork, and in the end so completely loses perspective that he imagines his own handiwork to be nobler than the creative plan which framed the universe.

Of course, materiality did not begin in the twentieth century, but it certainly received its greatest impetus in the last thirty years. Never before in known history has the whole race so completely objectified; never before have all classes of humanity been so completely dedicated to the perpetuation of physical standards. To summarize this thought, twentieth century metaphysics is, to say the least, in an uncongenial atmosphere. It is like a small tender plant in a bed of weeds. Up to the depression of 1929 "successful" men and women were amassing fortunes and piling up estates for heirs to squander. Wealth became the emblem of integrity. Life was an experience in high finance, a game played with dollars upon a checkerboard of years. There seemed to be a popular superstition to the effect that men could build a pyramid of profits that would reach the heavens. Then like the Tower of Babel, the whole structure collapsed and nothing but confusion remained. The year 1929 will long be remembered as the year of the great disillusionment.

Now to go back to the dawn of civilization. The occult sciences emerge from the night of time as the foundation of all knowledge and all culture.

For thousands of years, the Wisdom Teachings dominated all codes of human action and relationship. Inordinate human ambition was held in check by the powerful hierophants of the sacred Mysteries. All the evils we now suffer from existed in these remote times, but they were held in check so that they could never dominate the general course of action. There has always been perversion but while the Mystery Schools remained, perversion could never frame the laws of nations or dominate the policies of rulers. Religion was the moderator of extremes. It curbed excesses and demanded standards of conduct from the great as well as the lowly.

Education was the instrument by which ancient religion maintained its policies. No man could attain to a position of leadership or authority without passing through the institutions of spiritual education. Rulership by the informed is certain to be more adequate and enlightened than rulership by the uninformed. No man without reverence for the gods, veneration for life and understanding of nature could reach an estate where he exercised influence over the destinies of others.

A considerable percentage of rulers have always been corrupt, as individuals and tyrants frequently usurped the thrones of the weak, but the integrity of the mass of humanity was not greatly affected until materialism dominated the policies of empire. Materiality is the root of confusion, discord and dissension, and materiality increased to the degree that usurpation destroyed the power of the religious hierarchies in the state.

By the end of the third century of the Christian era the great metaphysical institutions of antiquity had almost entirely died out in European civilization. A perverse theology, which had lost the keys to its own mysteries, conspired with a corrupt political structure to bring about the enslavement of the minds and bodies of peoples and classes. With the exception of small groups of comparatively isolated thinkers. Western civilization was without an adequate mystical tradition for nearly 1600 years. During these long centuries of theological and political corruption religion degenerated from a spiritual force to an ecclesiastical bigotry. Theological history through the Dark Ages consists principally of reformations and inquisitions, and emerges into the light of modern times as a cycle of conscientious objections. Of course, 1600 years of theological corruption could scarcely end in anything but agnosticism and atheism. In the end, the thinking part of humanity rejected the only God they knew and began interpreting the universe from a mechanistic standpoint.

The 19th century brought the harvest. Science overthrew the dogmas of the church, and emerging triumphantly from two centuries of speculation, assumed the patriarchal role, promising to lead bewildered humanity into the Promised Land.

The fathers of science differed from their modern representatives in one important particular. They were mostly devout men rebelling not against religion as a spiritual necessity but theology as a material limitation. Science plays a very interesting part that is generally overlooked. It is through science that the Mystery Teaching came back to Europe and America.

The pioneers of science, having emancipated their minds from bondage to ecclesiastical authority, were free to explore not only the wonders of the universe, but the thoughts and beliefs of other thinkers of other times and beliefs. Religiously a pagan was a heretic, but science was not impressed by theological pronouncements. The result was that such names as Plato, Aristotle, and Euclid were restored to the consciousness of the race. Copernicus and Galileo, Newton and Kepler, Bacon and Descartes acknowledged their indebtedness to the ancients. Nor was it possible to long study the sciences of antiquity without becoming aware of the philosophies of antiquity. Science and philosophy must flourish together, for it is not possible to be deeply informed in one without an equal understanding of the other. Geographers looked back to Ptolemy; historians honored Herodotus; medicine recognized Hippocrates; philosophy paid homage to Plato; and natural science became definitely Aristotelian.

The scientific mind in the 17th and 18th century was both hungry and alert. Intellect, long in bondage to blind faith and adamantine dogma, rejoiced in the experience of freedom. There was an avid quest for every kind of knowledge. Nor were laymen alone in their desire to learn. The church itself became more alert. Science was first tolerated then embraced. Theology did not realize that the scientific attitude must finally bring down to a common ruin the arbitrary tenets of orthodoxy.

In the church itself appeared such men as Kircher, Melanchthon, Roger Bacon and Raymond Lully. These men combined a proper piety with an inquisitive reason. A man cannot escape the modifying influence of his own thinking. One cannot study great matters without growing a little. Ignorance was the fad of the Dark Ages. Scholarship became the fad of a more enlightened time. For centuries it was regarded as inelegant to be capable of reading and writing, and princes avoided education as they would the plague. By the close of the 18th century most aristocratic families had private museums and libraries, and a nobleman who did not retain a curator for his collection was utterly déclassé.

As early as the beginning of the 17th century, the mystical opinions of the ancients made a successful bid for popular favor. Several sects sprang up, essentially pagan in character. The magical arts revived, and Egyptian mysticism and the theurgical arts of the Neo-Platonists came to be regarded with ever-increasing favor. Theology stormed and pronounced, driving the heretical sects into secrecy where they continued to flourish on the fringe of respectability.

The loose ends of the mystical tradition were finally brought together under the name of Freemasonry, but in the 17th and 18th centuries many strange rites and curious rituals passed under that name. In France, Germany and England, particularly in France, Freemasonry, in its earlier forms, was a strange composite of partly digested fragments of Hindu, Egyptian, Persian, Greek and Jewish metaphysical speculations. The furor lasted for a full two hundred years, but by the beginning of the 19th century, the excitement had pretty well died down. Freemasonry had integrated into a fraternal order which no longer emphasized its kinship with the mystical tradition. The democratic psychology was dominating the popular mind. Men were experimenting with the feeling of being free and equal and their first instinct was towards becoming equal to the great and the wealthy. The urge to power and prosperity became the sustaining impulse. The obscure was forgotten, the evident was exploited, and European and American Civilization settled down to the development of the competitive instinct.

In this same century, science developed its sophistication. Scientists began to regard themselves as a race apart. By the middle of the 19th century, nearly all of the departments of science were suffering from an infallibility complex. To the scientist, wise in his own conceits, all that was not science was superstition. Both mysticism and the orthodox church fell under the general disapproval of the scientifically minded. Agnosticism was the new fad. Unfortunately, the fads of the schooled become the law of the unthinking. The whole race grew proud of its unbelief's. Science viewed itself as a spirit of emancipation. It resolved to save mankind from all the evils of beliefs, either good or bad, and establish humanity upon the solid rock of skepticism.

Darwin and Huxley were the demigods of the new era and their solemn pronouncements on everything in general became the gospel of the proletariat. By this time, science viewed ancient authority as a poor relation and excommunicated the illustrious ancients from its honor roll. Like a self-made man, science became ashamed of its own origin.

But extremes of thought are seldom comfortable codes to live by. It soon became evident that materialism was unsafe as a social program. The atheist generally has a hard time getting along with himself and a still harder time getting along with fellow atheists. Remove ideals and principles and nothing remains but exploitation, or at least a definite impulse in that direction. Before the 19th century, was fifty years old man's sense of proportion restored the mystical equation. The occult returned in the only form possible under the circumstances—spiritualism. To the self-satisfied materialist, smug in his unbelief's, psychical phenomena presented itself as a thorn in the flesh. Spiritualism struck at the very crux of the realist theory—the continuity of consciousness after death. Spiritualism divided the ranks of science almost immediately and there is no other department of occultism with which so many eminent scientists have aligned themselves. Furthermore, the principle underlying spiritualism was a principle which all normally minded human beings wanted to believe. We must clearly distinguish between spiritualism as a philosophical premise and spiritualism as a group of people sitting in the dark with a medium waiting for a table to tilt. Spiritualism as a philosophy is a demonstration of the continuity of consciousness after death. The idea, of course, raised general objection and was persecuted by the materialist on one side and the theologian on the other. But evidence is stronger than argument and spiritualism, though badly shaken in its early years, survived. It was the opening wedge and through the breach thus made the occult doctrines flooded back to the popular consciousness.

In the last half of the 19th century, idealism restated itself among most classes of people. Of course, scientists and the institutions which they dominate have held out to the bitter end. The death blow to material science was struck when scientists were forced to acknowledge psychology and came face to face with the factor of the subconscious mind.

In America, the mystical renaissance flowed through three widely divergent personalities. Albert Pike revised the higher degrees of Freemasonry, restoring a considerable part of the occult tradition concealed for centuries in its symbolism. Mary Baker Eddy caused the largest schism in the Christian church since the Protestant Reformation, and Madame Helena Blavatsky gave the Ancient Wisdom back to the modern world between the covers of the Secret Doctrine. The close of the 19th century found organized groups of mystics, metaphysicians and new thoughtists functioning in almost every important community of the civilized world. Great credit should go to those who pioneered in the field of metaphysics in the last century. They struggled against terrific odds of prejudice and selfishness, but they brought about a condition of free thought which we all enjoy in religious and philosophical matters today.

The opening years of the 20th century moved in a slow and even tempo. Men lived very much as they had but the intensity of recent years had not touched the average life. The period of the World War must be regarded as the turning point in the psychology of the century. This upheaval destroyed many of the standards and most of the illusions of previous years. There was a definite stimulus to all branches of metaphysical thought after the war. Spiritualism was the comfort of many who had lost dear ones in the catastrophe. Those of deeper mind, not interested merely in phenomena, sought for a philosophy of life which would explain so great a disaster without involving the integrity of divine law. Popular metaphysics as we know it today was distinctly an aftermath of the World War. Hundreds of thousands of bereaved persons searching for comfort and understanding and the courage to build a new world out of the chaos presented an opportunity for exploitation too great for the commercially-minded citizenry to resist. It is at this point then that we must concern ourselves with pseudo-metaphysics, a calamity in itself and a menace to thousands of sincere but inadequately informed persons.

Between 1918 and 1929, metaphysical and psychological shysters impoverished the popular purse to the tune of millions. One man who started life as an unsuccessful veterinary netted over a million a year for several years and finished up by a grand sale of non-existent red estate. His present whereabouts is somewhat obscure. Each of these shysters had disciples, many of them sincere people not knowingly a party to a fraud. They have continued on, sincerely enough, trying to teach worthless doctrines to an ignorant humanity. It will be a long time before we recover entirely from the metaphysical racketeering which flourished in the decade from 1920 to 1930. Literally hundreds of fantastic and worthless cults grew and flourished in an atmosphere of tragedy and deceit.

It must be definitely understood that the perpetrators of false doctrines were entirely without foundation in the true teachings of ancient philosophy. Several of the most successful of these pseudo teachers were entirely uneducated and unread. Success was due to showmanship and audacity. Practically all of the teachings were home-made, arising in minds totally unfit to direct the spiritual destiny of anything. One "successful teacher" founded a nation-wide program that netted a fortune upon thirty minutes reading in the public library, and the book, he read was itself the product of an imposter.

Nearly every race and accent were represented during these hectic years. Turbans, robes, whiskers and dress suits all joined in the program of super-salesmanship. "Peace, power and plenty" was the motto. The halt, the lame and the blind followed the piper. Clerks and stenographers, unhappy husbands and dissatisfied wives, the old and the young, the widows and the orphans struggled together to breathe, concentrate, affirm, meditate and eat their way to "peace, power and plenty." It was a sad story with a sad ending.

It would naturally follow that such a fantastical spectacle brought the whole subject of metaphysics and occultism into disrepute. The psychological circus however came to an end with the depression and the places where the hoodwinked gathered knew them no more. It was evidently useless to preach prosperity where there wasn't any, and besides this, a great many people were losing faith in the idea of wealth. It no longer looked like the will of heaven that all men should be opulent. A few of the more resourceful of the shysters moved into the field of dietetics, but the majority of them simply vanished away.

The metaphysical charlatan of today represents a post-graduate from the more obvious practices of years gone by. He is more subtle and more experienced, and, unfortunately for the public, he is better informed. Several very sincere groups of occultists have been promulgating their doctrines in this country for the last twenty-five years. These groups have been no part of the swindle of the 20's but have continued on their way, patiently and silently trying to educate thoughtful people in spiritual values. The sincerity of these groups deserves our admiration and respect. But for some reason, probably human nature, they have been unable to ground their followers, generally speaking, in the principle of discrimination. The result is there are many thousands of good, honest, well-meaning occultists who have studied rounds and races, reincarnation and karma for the last forty years. It is in this field and among these classes that the more polished fakers of today are shouting their wares. It has occurred to me that the average "old student" of metaphysics has a vulnerable point, in his armament as fatal as the heel of Achilles. Nearly all "old students" are waiting breathlessly for initiation or illumination and it is this weakness that leads them from the straight and narrow way to wisdom. We all long for the green pastures and we all like to think we are worthy to wander in the Elysian Fields even when we know that our worthiness is far from sufficient.

In viewing the occult problem as it is today, we must admit that most of the charlatans in the field are comparatively clever people. A novice would have great difficulty in detecting the fraud. Even experience in the general art of living will do little good. Nothing can save a prospective dupe except a thorough knowledge of occult matters. The average person is in no position to prove the authenticity of an occult organization, nor is he equipped to weigh the validity of one against another. How is he to know whether the moving power behind some belief is an adept or a clever crook? To those on the inside, values are rather evident but to the layman under the glamour of some mystical belief, the way of discrimination is hard.

One thing, however, is a help to the uninformed. The occult faker nearly always overplays his hand. His pretenses are too glamorous, his authority is too absolute, his promises are too spectacular. To sum it up, he is too, too divine! Honest men promise little and fulfill their promises, but dishonest men promise everything and deliver nothing.

Somewhere I have read an old philosopher who said, "Wise men speak of God but foolish men speak for God." This is also true when the subject is Mahatmas.

As Aristotle has said, "All men naturally desire to know," but as experience has proved, all men are not worthy to know Most human beings are but children in matters of the spirit and like children they need conscientious and intelligent guidance. It is difficult to give this guidance at the present time because every department of spiritual thought is dominated by policies, prejudices and profits. We are in a generation dedicated to material accomplishment and those who desire to perpetuate the mystic teachings must be indeed as wise as serpents.

With this preamble established in the mind, we can now approach the direct answering of the question stated at the beginning of this letter. In fact, what we have already set forth is itself a partial answer to the question.

Most metaphysically-minded people of today have turned to the occult science for solutions to vital problems of individual and collective life. The orthodox churches are incapable of satisfying the questioning type of mind. This is not a generation of blind faith and unquestioning belief. Too often, however, the step from orthodoxy to occultism is like jumping out of the frying pan into the fire. Popular occultism, like popular theology, is superstition ridden. If anything, the hazards of occultism are greater than the hazards of theology. Orthodoxy is one rather narrow set of beliefs that have grown familiar and somewhat comfortable from long usage. The term occultism covers a chaos of notions. A few itinerant teachers have isms and osophys of their own, hopelessly and horribly original. The sincere but uninformed seeker after truth, departing from the smugness of his old opinions, plunges into a sea of doubts. He is unequipped mentally for the task of discrimination, for he has long been a sheep in a thoughtless flock. Cast upon his own resources, he is most apt to end in a state of hopeless confusion.

As we have observed in previous letters, the average man is not built for mental exercise. For years, his church has done his thinking for him in religious matters. He is content with the realization that baptism has assured him salvation. The true doctrines of occultism are so diametrically opposed to such a concept that they offer small satisfaction to the lazy theologian. His natural tendency is to hunt for short cuts and easy methods in the same way that the frugal housewife goes from store to store in search of basement bargains. The housewife is always hoping that she is going to find "something for nothing" and the superficial student of metaphysics suffers from the same type of optimism.

Probably the truest slogan of this industrial era is "buyer beware." Life is beset by a tempting diversity of swindles. We have grown cautious from bitter experience. When we buy merchandise, we demand products from reputable firms. When we consult a lawyer, we like to know his standing and how many cases he has won. When we visit a doctor, we are deeply impressed by his credentials and engage him on the basis of his experience and excellence. But all too often in our search for spiritual values, we throw discrimination to the winds and waste our time on some fantastic character with soulful eyes, of whose integrity and ability, if any, we are entirely ignorant. In religion as in industry—let the buyer beware.

Another interesting point should be emphasized. Religious ignorance is the most difficult of all forms of ignorance to clear up because it is closely allied with the irrationalities of the emotional life. A bad mathematician can with practice cure his weakness; so can poor spellers or insufficient linguists, but a person suffering from religious ignorance is not only entirely oblivious of his limitations but is generally proud of them, resisting fanatically any effort to improve his state. Also, if you interfere with his convictions, no matter how stupid or malicious they may be, you are trespassing upon his inalienable right to freedom of worship and belief. You can call him ignorant in any of the branches of the arts, sciences or trades and he will likely agree with you, but if you tell him that his religious viewpoints are without a semblance of sanity he will rise in righteous wrath and hate you until the end of his days.

Yet if you pin one of these zealots down and demand of him what he actually knows about philosophy, transcendentalism, mysticism, magic, metaphysics and new thought, he will probably not be able to give you even a reasonably good definition of any one of these terms. He is full of convictions but his notions hang on such a shaky framework that they would be regarded as utterly worthless in any department of accredited scholarship. Perfectly certain of everything and utterly uninformed on nearly everything, enthusiastic, well-meaning metaphysicians are a hard class of people to work with. There is a "falling sickness" in metaphysics. When you really begin to congratulate yourself that you have helped a student on to a reasonable foundation of common sense, he proceeds to fall completely and ignominiously for the next shyster that comes along. Not once, but ad infinitum. The process of trying to extricate the student from the results of his own stupidity must then begin all over again.

To take a general view of the situation. There are at least several hundred metaphysical teachers in this country. Most moderate sized communities have at least one and in large cities there may be from a dozen to fifty or more. These constitute the resident class. In most cases their followings are small and audiences are of parlor proportions. Even when these teachers are representatives of national or international movements, they are almost certain to be promulgating some private revelation of their own. The majority of these resident metaphysicians have been pupils of some itinerant new thoughtist who passed through the community and held "most esoteric" classes for "old souls." After "the master" departs the disciple comes into his own. Mrs. Brown hangs out her shingle as a soul culturist and carries on Professor Blodgett's "work" as long as anyone in the community is willing to be worked. Mrs. Brown's pupils carry on in their turn, punctuating the original teachings of Blodgett-Brown with revelations and soul experiences of their own. As soon as a class of a dozen or more is formed, politics creeps in and the order splits under several new headings and so on until in the end the whole infirmity collapses of its own weakness.

It would be wrong to deny that many of these little metaphysical groups are devoutly sincere. They struggle on from year to year trying to support by their own sincerity an idea that is absolutely not worth supporting. Occasionally there is a brilliant exception but for the most part the subject matter is platitude and mediocrity.

In addition to the resident metaphysician, there is the ever ebbing and flowing tide of itinerants. One of the most famous of these wandering new thoughtists who gained international publicity once observed that they passed through the major cities of this country just often enough to "pick the lemons when they were ripe." These constitute the real metaphysical racketeers, but their tribe is waning under the pressure of hard times.

A metaphysical center in a flourishing community is little short of a bedlam. When the procession of visiting speakers is supplemented by the local would-bes, you have doctrines that are hair-raising to say the least. It is amazing how much nonsense can be crammed between four walls, and how many sincere people wander about in a daze, trying to orient themselves in a chemistry of yogi breathing, prosperity platitudes and realization circles. Is it any wonder then, that our metaphysicians have a somewhat vague and impractical air about them? Most of them are sinking for the third time in an ocean of conflicting beliefs.

It is to wonder how metaphysics has flourished in this country for so long without any definite organization taking place within it. The government has elaborate mechanism to prevent the capitalization of fraud, but law is wary against becoming involved in religious problems. One popular psychologist, pressed by the government to explain the disappearance of a large amount of funds, drew himself up and taking an air of martyred innocence declared that the whole matter was between himself and his God. Metaphysical students in this country must certainly number into the millions, yet no effort whatsoever has been made to standardize occult and metaphysical teaching upon any basis of integrity. Small groups have tried but their efforts were insufficient in the face of a prevailing chaos. The old Mystery Schools have disappeared from the view of the profane. The average student has no idea whatsoever as to what the original Schools actually taught and therefore cannot clearly and legally refute false doctrines.

Of course, the average shyster is too clever to acknowledge himself as the source of his doctrine. He speaks glibly and passingly of Himalayan brothers, Egyptian secrets, and then palms off any absurdity which he believes might prove profitable to himself. Overwhelmed by the emotional inference of high authority, innocent people are rapidly involved in teachings that can never prove anything but detrimental.

This exposition is not intended as an attack upon occultism but rather upon the abuses which are practiced under the name. The genuine occult tradition is the oldest, deepest and most complete revelation of divine mysteries that has been given to the race. In every generation a few sincere and enlightened thinkers, realizing the significance of this doctrine as a world-redeeming force, have sought to restore the Ancient Wisdom for the betterment of humanity. The Western descent of adepts is rather clearly defined. To mention a few illustrious names we have Roger Bacon, Giordano Bruno, Basil Valentine, Paracelsus, Sir Francis Bacon, St. Germain and Helena Blavatsky. Anyone familiar with the teachings of these occultists can easily understand that there is little in common between them and the pseudo metaphysicians who plague the present generation. Yet very few people know Paracelsus, other than as a name, if they know that. Totally unacquainted with the bona fide teachings, the uninformed student is easily deceived by inferior and irrelevant revelations.

Someone may ask where do false teachings come from? There are only two answers. Self-deceit or fraud. Hallucinations have all too frequently given rise to religious doctrines in this troubled world. Mediumship, psychical experiences, ill-digested reading and a vivid imagination may cause a perfectly sincere person to believe that he is the one and only possessor of universal truth. Or he may be the sincere dupe of the fraud of another. Fraud has innumerable origins, all stimulated by the hope of profits. A mysterious manner and a ready tongue work wonders with the ignorant.

Of course, if a doctrine is false and lacks the elements of truth and integrity, it cannot convey these elements to the student. The thousands of impractical, wool-gathering, inconsistent people who give new thought a bad name are mostly victims of fraud whose lives have been unbalanced by attempting to live or even believe doctrines intrinsically false. True occultism never made anyone impractical, but pseudo-occultism or the incapacity to understand and appreciate occult facts—these will lead to a disordered life.

(To be continued next month)

Sincerely yours,

Manly P. Hall

MARCH 1, 1936

Dear Friend,

In the preceding letter l think we have fairly well established the causes for the general lack. of consistency evident in the thoughts and actions of the great majority of metaphysicians... We must next consider some of the less obvious factors which contribute to the general disorder in the sphere of the occult sciences. Poise is the outward expression of inward equilibrium.

Poise cannot manifest where there is inward inconsistency. The average person suffers from psychic stress, that is there is distinct inharmony between code and conduct, between impulse and action. For the most part religious movements ignore the factor of psychic stress. This is because psychology is not generally included in the theological or metaphysical curriculum. Of course, the word psychology is a comparatively recent invention, but the system of facts which the term psychology has been coined to cover has existed since the beginning of human consciousness.

Stress and strain in the bodily economy result in nerve tension and this in turn contributes a powerful impulse to erratic thought and action. Most modern religious movements, whether orthodox or heterodox, are of the "listen and accept" type. The followers think, what they are told to think, read, what they are told to read, and attempt to act as they are told to act, usually failing miserably in the sphere of action. Religious hysteria is due to psychic stress and metaphysical hysteria has the same cause. Until this problem of internal maladjustment is solved, reasonableness and poise will be lacking in the material sphere.

There are two primary causes of psychic stress—inconsistency and contradiction. Inconsistency is an interruption in the flow of energy from cause to effect, and contradiction is a confliction of several dissonant factors which set up irritation in the subjective nature. Both inconsistency and contradiction are very frequently found in the make-up of the modern metaphysician. Inconsistency arises from inward causes; contradiction usually arises from outward factors. A person who does not act in accordance with his belief or his knowledge is guilty of inconsistency, and a person who wanders from one belief to another without properly digesting any of these beliefs is guilty of contradiction.

As contradiction is the simplest and most obvious of the causes of psychic stress, we shall consider that first. Contradiction is most apt to arise from an effort to be broad-minded or liberal, tolerant or generous in religious attitudes. While it is a virtue to respect the opinions of others, it is not always a virtue to try to live or accept these contradictory opinions in your own life. While it is a philosophical truism that all religions are divinely inspired and all great systems of philosophy are established in spiritual truths, the modern disciple must remember that all institutionalized religions have suffered numerous corruptions of beliefs The result is that while all the great world religions may arise from the same truth and be utterly united in principle, they are now hopelessly divided from one another by dogmas, bigotries and misunderstandings. When the average person, therefore, attempts the study of a religion he is probably not studying a religion at all but merely interpretations, often narrow and conceited, which have crept into the religion during its centuries of function. Conflicting dogmas have resulted in a war of faiths. Institutionalized religions are organized on competitive standards and the sublime mystical truths upon which the religion was built are relegated to obscurity. It is for this reason that the attempt to live all beliefs leads not to illumination but to contradiction and psychic stress.

If this is true of the great world religions, it is even more true of the thousands of little sects which make up metaphysics. Many of these sects are founded on nothing but deceit or fraud and the effort to live several of them at the same time is entirely disastrous to poise. Few students of occultism realize what it means to change beliefs in the middle of life. To be guilty of the indiscretion of monthly or annual religious turn-abouts is hazardous to life and sanity. Every belief has a vibration of its own and the acceptance and living of that belief builds this vibration into the life and consciousness of the disciple. If, a few months later, he changes his belief he not only changes his mind but causes a complete vibratory readjustment in his superphysical parts. This adjustment is not made quickly. There is always psychic stress and the whole system is put under a heavy strain.

The cultist, always looking for something new and following every itinerant metaphysician, is inwardly a conglomeration of discords. Sets of vibrations are superimposed upon each other so rapidly that his psychic serenity is entirely shattered. Outwardly he may only feel a little confused, but inwardly he is a wreck. As poise and discrimination come from within, he rapidly loses his ability to assert these virtuous temperance's. Inwardly he is a tumbling ground for notions, and outwardly he is a nervous wreck.

The more sincerely a student has studied a line of thought, the more of a shock a change of religious foundation will be to him. This is especially true if the new belief is of a lower rate of vibration than the one he previously held. I personally know a number of people who have affiliated themselves with a dozen or more religious, metaphysical or new thought organizations in as many years. With them "joining" is a sort of experiment. They figure that if they like it, they will stay. Then along comes another belief a little more fantastic, and they flock to that. These people regard themselves as "old souls." The soul however is not old, it is merely decrepit from psychic stress. In religious matters, the student is better off if he will attach himself to a sincere, unostentatious and reasonable system of belief and remain with it. He may make a mistake by so doing, but if he remains personally honest, it will not be a serious mistake. On the other hand, if he joins a number of sects, he will make several mistakes and they will all be serious.

There is a point here which is a little difficult to make, but is very important. Religious broadmindedness arises not from much joining but from much understanding. When the disciple becomes inwardly aware of the spiritual truths which underlie religion, he will then discover that he is one with all faiths, not because he has joined them all but because he has inwardly perceived the truth which sustains them all. In the East there is a fable concerning this. The story is of a man who tried to understand a tree by counting its leaves. He finally discovered that all the leaves grew upon a single trunk and that if he understood the trunk or the tree as a whole, he was instantly able to sense the proper significance of each of the leaves. Religion is like a tree. The sects and creeds are like the branches and leaves of the tree. We discover the nature of the tree not by studying the leaves and branches alone, but by becoming rationally aware of the significance of the whole tree. The moment we become truly religious, there is a place in our appreciation for all cults and all sects, but we do not rush in a frantic effort to join them all. Religion is one, creeds are many, but he who possesses religion is master of all creeds.

In every large community, there is a division of metaphysicians, the less rational type who constitute the guild of the "joiners." They flow instinctively into every new cult which comes along. They are the flotsam and jetsam of occultism, always in the front row, but so scattered and disorganized mentally that they are incapable of learning and incapable of sensing their own stupidity. Of all people studying metaphysics, these most of all need help, but they are the hardest to help. They are a discredit to the whole field of metaphysics and are the distinct product of avid incapacity. The sincere student must avoid assiduously any contamination from contact with the chronic joiner. The end of the trail is psychic demoralization. The metaphysical addict may be as much of a problem as the drug addict or the alcoholic. The moral is, when in doubt about an organization, do not join. When uncertain, do not fly to some cult to be fleeced, but retire into your own self and ponder deeply upon an intelligent course of action. Apply the ounce of prevention and escape from a host of disillusionments.

The other cause of psychic stress is inconsistency and this is an entirely personal problem which each truth-seeker must work out for himself. It is the strict harmonizing of belief and action and offers the most difficult task that confronts the would-be disciple of esoteric teachings. Man fails to be spiritually honest because of the interval between knowledge and works. There is an old saying that we all know better than we do. The man who desires to be superior to other men can only truly achieve this end by being nobler than other men in thought and action. There is no other superiority acceptable to bona fide metaphysics. Psychic stress due to inconsistency must be overcome by a twofold correction. The inward standards must be put in order first and the outward life must then be brought into perfect harmony with these standards. This may sound like hard work and it is, the most difficult work in the world. But when a man asks for wisdom, he asks for the greatest treasure that the universe possesses and he must be prepared to pay for it with a high and noble intensity of purpose.

Our first problem then will be putting the inner standard in order. Of course, in particular, this adjustment is an individual matter, but in general it follows certain universal laws which can be accepted without modification in the majority of cases. There is a very confused code of spiritual values in the Western world. The average metaphysician's inner conviction is a sort of potpourri of theological, scientific and metaphysical notions. A little of hell-fire and damnation theology clings to the subconscious mind of the majority of people who have grown up through a theological generation. This fundamental premise is modified by other opinions based upon reading, thinking, and experience. In very few lives, however, is the spiritual standard clear, clean-cut and reasonable. In many it is a hazy mass of hopes, wishes and other weak ingredients. In many metaphysicians, it is a conflict of several standards due to dabbling in divergent philosophic or religious systems. The worst fault, however, arises from over-estimation of personal virtue and integrity. Good, well-meaning folk who are just gradually coming to a state where they are reasonable human beings suffer from the delusion that they are on the verge of divinity, and establish standards for themselves so entirely beyond their capacity that life becomes a painful span of struggle and failure.

Regarding the follies of life, Socrates is attributed with the very sage remark; "Tor the foolish excess, for the informed moderation, and for the gods abstinence." One of our troubles seems to be a general over-estimation of our own importance. We dream that we are gods but we are men and the result is that our earthy part rebels against our mental temper and there is chaos in our world.

A spiritual standard, to be practical for the average person, must be within the sphere of possibility, in fact it should be well within. Of course, we should strive to be better than we are. That is taken for granted. In striving, however, the goal should not be so remote that despair alone will crown the effort. Before great virtues come little virtues, and it has been our observation that most metaphysicians who are striving after great virtues are woefully lacking in the smaller ones. It is natural that man should associate religion with distant, sublime and unapproachable realties. But it is also prudent that the intelligent man should associate the thought of religion with gradual, constant improvement in small matters. Only those who are faithful in the little things shall be made master over greater things. The psychical conflict between spiritual standard and material action will be greatly mitigated by reforming the inward standard to a code of moderation. Man, a naturally immoderate animal, will find enough work for the present life trying to bridle the beast within. Moderation of standard must arise finally from the individual himself, wisely estimating a standard of moderation suitable for himself. I have observed many sincere people brought to misery, sickness and even death because they had never intelligently moderated their standards of action.

The first work of moderation is, of course, to avoid extremes. One of the simplest forms of extremism is fad. Bad-minded people have one of the most serious diseases in the world because they are gradually rendered incapable of moderation. A good approach to moderation is to moderate extremes of feeling so that tranquility gradually dominates the emotional excess. If this is accomplished a serious cause of emotional unbalance is removed. Tranquility takes a normal attitude towards everything. One by one, the vice must be tempered. Not killed out at first, but moderated. Once the temperament is brought to moderation, the excesses gradually die out of themselves and do not require any desperate effort to destroy them. As the Gita has wisely observed: "Only the man who is balanced in pain and pleasure is fitted for immortality." Look about you among people whom you know to be interested in metaphysical subjects, look within yourself, and then frankly ask the question: are these others and myself balanced in pain and pleasure, unmoved by the excesses that destroy the tranquility of the unenlightened? If you perceive, as you most certainly will, a general lack of balance and tranquility, then the life work is clearly indicated, for there is no accomplishment in great things until these lesser problems have been met and mastered.

As you look among truth seekers, you will find generally a rather admirable, well-meaning and sincere group of people. But one is a gossip, another is jealous, a third has a bad temper, a fourth has "psychic experiences" and the fifth cannot stop talking. It is probable that most new thoughtists are law-abiding citizens, not guilty of major crimes, but nearly all of them guilty of dispositions, some of them rather nasty. Yet, completely oblivious of these dispositions, these "disciples" continue in their quest for illumination, making little if any effort to put themselves right with themselves. Of course, the result of searching without first mastering self is to come up against a blank wall. No person is capable of achieving inward illumination while the disposition remains unconquered. Many know this but have solaced themselves with the fond illusion that they will find truth in spite of their temperaments and in spite of their vices. This is a sort of psychical hang-over from the doctrine of eleventh-hour conversions and vicarious atonements that is constantly getting in the way of honesty.

Having established a code of moderate purpose in the inner life, attention should next be turned to the body or the outer life, the other polarity of the problem. Of course, the body of itself does nothing except digest, assimilate and excrete. All other functions are bestowed upon it by the superphysical disposition. Any evil which the body apparently performs is really to be attributed to emotional or intellectual excess within the body. On the other hand, through the body, man contacts the outer world, and the external sphere is truly man's testing place. Here, he must live outwardly with his inner convictions against what seems to be an organized opposition. The proof of man's sufficiency, however, is not that he conquers the world but rather that the world does not conquer him. He cannot remake the universe, but he can prevent outward conditions from destroying his inner character. This is his problem. Right must survive in the presence of a material adversary. Only where man has reached a high degree of personal development is he immune from the evils of organized society.

This is his initiation. He no longer descends into the crypts under the temples to fight wild beasts and master specters. Rather his test is that he shall live well in the presence of infinite opportunity to live badly, that he shall practice the virtues in the presence of the temptation to exploit the vices, that he shall achieve moderation while part of an intemperate social order. He shall not become a god among men; rather he shall become a man among beasts.

Having thus established the facts, which is not a difficult matter, for the factors are evident, we are confronted with what is truly called The Great Work—the living of the truth we know.

To define religion, we can say religion is the living of the highest practical spiritual standard. Actually, religion has little if anything to do with creeds or beliefs. It is the living of principle, and this one fact alone is the cornerstone of the house of spiritual science. In theory, we all agree on this; in practice, there is a wide divergence. Selfishness, narrowness, intolerance—these are the things that we perceive even while men tail; of their spiritual aspirations. Whenever we find a man talking of charity and brotherhood and at the same time living a mean standard of exploitation, we know that life is filled with psychic stress. To believe one thing and to do another is to contradict oneself, and this is a serious matter in the subjective life of the individual. Again, friction and dissonance are set up. Vibrations clash and conflict. Sickness and suffering are the inevitable result. No man can live outwardly on a level lower than his inward conviction and be happy. Karma sees to that. The interval of harmony becomes an avenging force, engendering a thousand reactionary ills. These reactions destroy poise and discrimination, producing the familiar scattered effect and numerous ailments of the nervous system. Inconsistency and contradiction, then, are important factors in the failure of integrity.

* * * * *

QUESTIONS AND ANSWERS

QUESTION—Please explain the Mystery of Omens.

ANSWER—Nearly all of the important events of history have been preceded by prophetic circumstances. Visions have appeared in the sky like the mysterious sword of flame that hung over Jerusalem before its fall. Curious accidents have occurred presaging evil, and coming events have presented themselves as dreams and visions. Nearly all the great changes of human affairs have followed appropriate warnings, and whole books have been written describing and proving the general occurrence of omens. Occultism explains the appearance of strange portents of approaching fate in a very simple way. All major changes in the physical life of man or his world are the effects of causes which exist not in the physical world but in the superphysical planes of the universe. An earthquake, for example, exists as an archetype or pattern in the invisible world long before the physical phenomenon takes place. Seismic cataclysms which will not occur in the material world for centuries already exist as archetypes in the superphysical body of the planet. These archetypes are established by the law of Karma and the force of them is built up by the repetition of the causes which originally precipitated the pattern. Let us say, for example, that Karma decrees that a continent and its inhabitants shall be submerged by volcanic forces. This fact having been metaphysically established, is intensified by the destructive tendencies in the life and action of the doomed people. At last, after centuries of crystallization, the archetypal pattern reaches such definite proportions that this psychical pattern moves the physical elements into agreement with the metaphysical design or shape. It follows that archetypes in the process of crystallization become more and more tangible or physical. The result is that mediums, psychics and other supersensitive persons may sense or see the archetype before the physical phenomenon is precipitated. Also, the increasing force building up in the archetype occasionally produces curious, unaccountable happenings. These happenings are not unlike the pranks played by electricity under certain conditions, for the force behind all archetypes is basically electrical, but a far more subtle form of electricity than can be recognized by material science. Premonitions are truly coming, events casting their shadows before them, because these events occur in the invisible world long before they can be felt in dense material forms. The archetypal ethers of the earth already carried locked within them the forms or patterns of all of the important changes that will take place geologically or socially for the next several thousands of years. The mind of man not only remembers the past but plans the future, and the intellectual substances of the earth already bear the thought patterns of a wide variety of changes and achievements. All of the inventions and as yet undiscovered secrets of nature are plainly existent in the archetypal sphere and it is from this world of patterns that men draw their discoveries, creations and compositions. Mozart once observed that every piece of music that he composed he actually heard as though played in the air by an invisible orchestra before he wrote it down. Many great inventions have come as visions and dreams, for under certain circumstances the creative type of mind can contact the sphere of archetypes where all things yet to be known exist as living pictures composed of vibrant ether.

QUESTION—Please have something to say on the subject of Diet.

ANSWER—From the earliest times religious institutions have regarded diet as an important aspect of spiritual culture. The systems of eating recommended by these various groups differ in some parts, but for the most part agree on the essential principles. All religious and philosophical schools have warned against over-eating as the worst of dietetic evils. Too much food and elaborate and complicated menus receive the weight of general censure. The Pythagoreans advised moderation and simplicity, and the followers of the school enjoyed extraordinary health and longevity. According to the tradition, Pythagoras himself, when nearly 100 years of age, had the strength and endurance of a youth in his twenties. Apollonius of Tyana, who followed the Pythagorean disciplines, was in his prime, physically and mentally, at the age of 100.

A reasonable viewpoint on this subject for modern consideration would emphasize the evil of excess, with one reservation. Diets for the philosophically minded should not be imposed upon growing children who require much more of food than persons of mature years. Over-feeding after middle life is particularly unfortunate, and it has been scientifically proven that the body survives longer on hunger than it does on satiety. The wise course is to discover the minimum upon which the body flourishes and adheres to it.

As to the nature of that which is to be eaten, there is less uniformity of belief. Various races have food staples which are accepted as indispensable, but again there is agreement that foods which undergo elaborate processes of refinement or cooking are to be avoided. Most religious diets work for energy-building foods with low starch content. Pythagoras advised grain, cheese, fruit and vegetables which mature above the ground, nor does he seem to have condemned the eating of meat. But he advised magistrates to refrain from eating meat for twenty-four hours previous to decisions in court, etc. for the sake of mental clarity.

Generally speaking, a moderate, well-balanced meal of natural foods is suitable for general use, but no elaborate departure should be made from eating habits without the assistance of a skilled dietitian. The various abnormalities of body chemistry present in nearly every person living in our peculiar social system should never be overlooked when planning a diet. Extensive fasting was discouraged among the more philosophic sects, although the entirely devout frequently starved themselves to death. If the amount of food necessary to the bodily economy is skillfully gauged, there is no need of fasting to clean out the system. Some of the old schools taught that the clarity of the reason was improved by abstaining from food one day each week and eating a normal amount the rest of the time. The Mohammedan fast of Ramadan was instituted as a physical aid to the spiritual life due to the rather intemperate eating of the Moslem world. There is no food panacea for the evils of the soul. No man shall reach heaven by dieting alone. The ability of the human being to function at a maximum of efficiency demands the proper fueling for his physical engine.

It has generally been observed that if a person interested in metaphysical matters uses a general moderation in his eating, the law of natural selection will gradually assert itself. A person doing intensive mental work will naturally rebel against the sluggishness caused by the over-eating of coarse low vibration foods. The diet will be corrected by the inward tendencies of the mind and life. Occasionally we meet a person who regards himself as a very advanced metaphysician who at the same time is wrestling with the diet demon. The fact is that no one highly advanced in metaphysical matters will have any such conflict. The diet will be determined not by the appetites but by the chemistry which philosophy has set up in the bodily organisms. Do not steel yourself against eating things which you believe are inconsistent with philosophy. Rather perfect the philosophy and you will find that natural selection will cause you to finally eat that which is useful to you. In the average person, unfortunately, the law of natural selection is obscured by the artificiality of the conditions under which we live. As Socrates so wisely observed: "Moderation is the cornerstone of the virtues." Nor should we forget the entirely significant words of the Nazarene teacher: "It is not that which goeth in at the mouth that defileth a man; it is that which cometh out of the mouth that defileth a man."

QUESTION—Is there any virtue in sleeping with the head to the north, south, east or west?

ANSWER—As all the occult mysteries have written, man is a miniature world and the magnetic currents of his body correspond with the vaster currents moving about and through the earth. It would naturally follow that if man harmonizes the direction of the flow of his own energies with the flow of the energies of the earth, he will avoid conflict between his own life and the life of the world. In the Northern hemisphere, it is proper to sleep with the head to the North so that the magnetic currents flow parallel with the spine. In the Southern hemisphere, the head should be to the South, and in the equatorial zone, the head should be to the East. Experimentation has proven that by following this rule rest is more perfect and in some cases, relief has been found for restless sleeping, confused dreams and insomnia. It would be wrong to say that failure to follow this rule would prevent sleep or endanger the individual, but there is a certain added benefit which results from cooperating with nature in every possible way. Of course, to sleep with one's head in the right direction does not produce spirituality. It merely increases body normalcy, in this way giving added vitality and efficiency which, through proper direction, may contribute to spiritual improvement.

QUESTION—Is it true that men should live much longer than most do at the present time?

ANSWER—A man of letters not long ago hazarded the opinion that, considering the length of time devoted to the periods of development and growth, the human being should live about four hundred years. Strangely enough, there is no historical example of a human being achieving this length of life in the last several thousands of years. Of course, in the metaphysical traditions we find records of what Thomas Vaughan, the Rosicrucian initiate, called "long livers," but the occult tradition is not accepted by modern science. There are records however, of men whose lives have exceeded 200 years, and a goodly number who have reached 150. China has produced an unusual number of very aged persons, and it might be well to consider some of the factors involved in the achievement of an unusual span of life.

Two factors, of course, immediately present themselves. In the first place, some achieve great age by virtue of constitution. The body seems to be born with an unusual capacity for endurance. The second factor is cultivation and discipline. By a certain program of carefully studied action, the natural span is increased and efficiency continued far beyond the generally accepted boundaries. The Chinese formula for longevity is extremely simple and has unusual merit in the light of our present uncertain generation. The Taoists of China, among whom are to be found a Host of centenarians, gave as the first key to extensive living the formula: do not worry. To use an old adage, most people use

up the second half of life in the first half. Excesses of emotion, inordinate ambitions, the psychological acceptance of responsibilities, attachments, and all the vast army of concerns which bow us down, carve huge slices from our later years. Every time we become fussed and bothered, we shorten life and destroy the tranquility of the years we do not destroy. In the Taoist belief, nothing is important. In their opinion, the worst thing that can happen to anyone is to die, and that is not important anyway. There is nothing worth fretting over or hastening after. Things you do not have are responsibilities escaped. High ran you cannot achieve is disaster avoided. Man's wants are many but his needs are few, and the Taoist maizes the goal of his life to live without effort, without stress and without strain. He moves slowly and methodically, without tension and without nerves to whatever end he desires to accomplish, always careful that his ends are few. If a Taoist, by some miracle, finds himself in a position of responsibility, his first task is to remove the consciousness of responsibility in himself. Wherever he is, he is unconcerned. He does everything as wisely as he can and then immediately dismisses the entire matter from his mind. Rich or poor, befriended or alone, old or young, he lives in the same sense of detachment. He wastes no energy and permits nothing to irritate him. In this way, he overcomes most of the causes of rapid decay.

Very few people wear out; most of them rot out. The life is corroded by acids of disposition. Strength is wasted towards ends that are not real or valuable. Most men die from the exhaustion attendant upon the effort to live. But the Chinese sage lives without effort. He seldom practices great physical exercise, in fact, he avoids every type of exertion. He never wonders about what he does or fears the results of his thoughts or deeds. He lives by a formula of right. He never departs from it and he never concerns himself with evils that may come to him. With this formula he may find himself hale and hearty at 150, frequently sought for advice, regarded as a paragon of the virtues, and entirely comfortable.

Another way of stating the Taoist formula is that every individual should be life water, for this fluid fits itself into any container without discomfort, flows into low and simple places without despair, and in the end mingles with the universal waters without regret. Placidity is power, relaxation is length of years, detachment is health. To sum up, it is only a Taoist or one of similar accomplishment who takes the sting out of life and is fitted to endure the years.

Sincerely yours,

MANLY P. HALL

SPECIAL ARTICLES

A considerable number of Mr. Hall's most interesting and important writings are available only in the form of magazine articles. The Phoenix Press, 944 W. 20th St., Los Angeles, is able to supply the following articles for a limited time. The price is 10 cts for each article, or $2.00 for the entire collection. Please send a list of those you desire, with your money order. The Portrait of Christian Rosencreutz; The Music of the Spheres; Freemasonry and the Osiris Myth; Atlantis, the Lost World; The Gnostic Cults; The City of the Gods; The Heavenly Fire; The Problem of Healing; A Retrospect of Races; The Mystery of the Feathered Serpent; Some Notes on Numerology; The Egyptian Initiate; Tibetan Cabalism; Odin, and the Odinic Mysteries; The Staff of Hermes; Character Analysis; Noah and His Wonderful Ark; Do We need the Mystery Schools; Faust, the Eternal Drama; Wands and Serpents; Krishna and the Battle of Kurukshetra; Freemasonry and Catholicism; The Book of Revelation; Occult Diseases; Japanese Buddhism; The Principles of Astrology; Superphysical Causes of Disease. Those purchasing the complete collection will receive with the above list, over 100 other articles by Mr. Hall including, The Initiates of the Flame; Occult Biographies, The Bacon-Shakespeare Controversy, etc. Less than a hundred copies remain. This will probably be the last opportunity to obtain these sets.

APRIL 1, 1936

Dear Friend,

QUESTION—Some metaphysical Teachers promise that through the study of their philosophy's students can evade the effects of certain natural laws such as Reincarnation and Karma; other metaphysical Teachers promise miracles of health and prosperity to their followers; and still others assure their disciples spiritual and material protection against the evils of life. Please clarify the relationship between codes of spiritual action and the material rewards arising from such action.

ANSWER—As we have explained in previous letters of this series, the field of popular metaphysics is now a battlefield of competitive isms. There is no code of fair play among the merchants of pseudo religion. Memberships are built up on the catch-as-catch-can policy. All is fair in love, war, and metaphysics. Many cults unquestionably set out on the ideas behind these movements are not big enough or substantial enough to command a general hearing or a wide acceptance. It is when faced with such a problem that metaphysical movements frequently sacrifice integrity upon the altar of success. It was once observed by a prominent businessman that it takes a great deal of advertising to sell an inferior product, and nearly all over-advertised products are inferior.

In metaphysical movements, two distinct types of organizations are easily distinguishable. The first is the comparatively sound and sensible type, which advertises modestly and holds its memberships together by the value of the instruction given and not by extravagant misstatements of fact. The other type of cult follows a business policy even more blatant than that of the patent medicine vendor of years gone by. The very business methods of such organizations should condemn them to reasonably minded people, but unfortunately in religious matters few people are reasonably minded. The business man does not expect miracles, but the metaphysician is always hoping for the impossible.

Fakery and elaborate promises always go hand in hand. Fakery generally follows the line of least resistance. Nearly all people want to be beautiful. In this department, metaphysics and cosmetics share the spoil. Nearly everyone wants to have a dominating, powerful, magnetic personality. Nearly everyone desires to be a citizen of distinction in his own community. The poor desire money, the moderately comfortable desire for wealth, and the wealthy desire more wealth. The sick want to be well, the lame, the halt and the blind want to be relieved of their infirmities. These desires taken together are a fertile field for an individual with the exploiting instinct. Fifty percent of the population of this country may be regarded as poor, and poverty is a terrible thing under an economic system which reserves practically all opportunity for the wealthy. No small proportion of the population may be accepted as suffering from some form of poor health, real or imaginary. Add to this the spiritual fact that nearly every living person has a bad conscience, and you can get some idea of the magnitude of the problem under consideration. Of course, all of the dissatisfied and the infirm are not within reach of the metaphysical spellbinder. Millions are intrenched behind the battlements of the various orthodox religious organizations, where incidentally, a good number of them are better off. Another considerably smaller block is secure behind an impregnable consciousness of materialism, a protected if uncomfortable position. It is safe to say from the records that have been kept, however, that there are between ten and twenty million people in America belonging to what may be termed a broadminded stratum. These people, most of them well meaning, but the majority utterly ignorant of the facts of life, are imposed upon year after year and deceived time after time, wasting time and money upon unimportant or fraudulent beliefs and doctrines.

But if fraud succeeds and reaps a golden harvest, all of the blame does not rest with fraud. A person stupid enough to be deceived, and waiting with an open purse for some fantastic personality to come along and fleece him, is certainly a party to the crime. People, fundamentally honest, in either material or spiritual matters, are not easily fooled. It is the streaky of dishonesty in human nature that makes fraud profitable. People desiring something they have not earned are almost certain to lose in their effort to get it. It is the stupidity and cupidity of millions that sustain corruption in every department of society, and religion cannot remain pure and undefiled while the men who make up the belief are in themselves corrupt.

Many metaphysicians have come to me with their tales of woe, of how they only wanted the Elixir of Life, the Philosopher's Stone, and the secret of eternal wealth; that it had been promised to them in ten easy lessons at the ridiculously low sum of twenty-five dollars, and that they had been viciously cheated by a nasty man who could not deliver the goods. The picture is extremely ludicrous unless you are the victim, then it is a dastardly disaster. While it is probably true that the misrepresenting "mystic" should be behind bars, it is also true that people fooled by such nonsense ought to be kept in a safe place also.

If a man says to you that he can stop the workings of Reincarnation and Karma, suggest that he first give you a practical demonstration of his ability by stopping the motion of the sun, or like Canute the Dane, seat him by the shore of the sea and order him to change the tides. Universal law is as immutable as the seasons, as inevitable as the course of the stars, and no metaphysical maestro is going to alter these inevitables in ten lessons or in ten million lessons. The law of cause and effect is as inevitable as day and night, as certain as the tides, and as constant as the ages. This law says that as ye sow, so shall ye reap. What you earn comes to you, what you have not earned can never be yours, and neither God nor man can alter the complexion of these facts. Universal laws are inevitable and the universe is never for one moment trusted to the keeping of the prophet, false or true.

There is no teaching more dangerous than that of special dispensation and special privileges. There are no such things in the universe and anyone claiming to be able to administer them is either self-deluded or fraudulent. If there be one thing constant in the universe, it is law. This law is the hope of the wise, the firm rock upon which the informed build their philosophy of life. It is a fatal day for the truth-seeker when he lets some pseudo-mahatma talk him out of the realization of universal integrity.

Now let us see something of the truth of the situation. What are the material results of a life dedicated to a spiritual code of action? Of course, we are referring now to a life. This does not mean a few weeks of instruction or ten simple lessons. It means exactly what the words themselves mean—a lifetime, year after year lived honestly and intelligently. A man is not spiritualized because he reads books, or because he studies with some famous teacher, even if that teacher is bona fide. He is not spiritual because he knows spiritual people, or because he recites a few platitudes morning and evening, or because he goes into the silence, or because he prays a formula, or because he chants Sanskrit, or because he pays dues to a metaphysical organization, or because he has been "initiated" into some mystical cult. He is only a spiritual person because year after year, he lives a spiritualized, philosophical life. There is an old saying common to the clergy, that the parishioners want to go to heaven on the coat-tails of the ministry, and there are a great many people who believe that their spiritual salvation is all worked out because they have joined an organization with advanced views, or because they believe in Reincarnation and Karma, or because they love animals. Some think they work out their eternal destiny with diet. Others strive to breathe their way into a divine state. Others use packages of appropriate herbs gathered by a "mahatma" on the top of the Himalayas, sold at a dollar a package to the believers. Religion is not a fancy process of mechanical exercises or affirmations. It is not something that you rub on. It is something you lure day by day. Religion is the improvement of the self by a constant course of self-discipline, called the philosophic life. It is something to be lived, not talked about; something to be practiced, not affirmed. The great metaphysical systems of the past have descended to us in a fragmentary condition due to the centuries of theological blight that nearly destroyed classical philosophy. Pythagoras and Plato were metaphysicians, so were Buddha and Confucius, but their metaphysics has little in common with the popular brand. The school of Pythagoras produced over a hundred and fifty great philosophers, men who conquered the physical life and rose sublimely above all of the limitations and illusions of the flesh.

To begin with metaphysics, actually, is not a popular belief. It is a system of thinking appropriate only to highly organized and highly trained minds. When the house wife wishes to become a metaphysician, she must realize that she is attempting a study that has taxed the capacity of the world's best organized intellects. She must approach her subject slowly, ready to give at least five or ten years to foundation work before she attempts to launch her unprepared intellect upon the vast ocean of learning. Metaphysics is for thinking people, and when the thoughtless take it up, then comes the deluge. This may make the whole subject seem very difficult and impossible and be a great discouragement to the optimistic, but it is far better that they be discouraged in the beginning than disillusioned later, after years of sincere and misspent effort. While the blind lead the blind in spiritual sciences, the great truths of nature appear only in distorted and unnatural forms.

To study metaphysics, in the hope of curing a stomachache, or of attaining cosmic consciousness, or increasing the income, is to be guilty of sacrilege to say the least, or possibly better, absurdity and effrontery. It is worse than binding the gods to the millstone of greed. The trouble with modern metaphysics is that the majority of so-called metaphysicians have not the slightest idea as to either the subject or its scope. An appropriate simile is difficult. We might say that metaphysics is a vast structure, a noble temple, with its footings in the foundation of the-universe and the vast arch of heaven itself its only roof. The ages have sought for truth. Hundreds of millions have lived to achieve it and millions have died for it. Heroes, martyrs, sages, saints and prophets, world Saviors and demigods of forgotten ages, are the priests of this great house. The gates of this sanctuary are to be approached only with reverence. The ancient road that leads to it is worn smooth with the footsteps of uncounted multitudes, and the modern metaphysician of today is so incapable of perceiving even dimly the immensity and sanctity of this science, that he confuses this divine program with a businessmen's cooperative luncheon club, or a local clinic.

The Ancient Wisdom offers nothing to a disciple of the Great Work but the opportunity to improve himself by a consistent program of intelligently directed effort. In the East, discipleship is a rigid discipline without reward or promise. No individual is ready for a religious or philosophical life while he has to be induced into the process of being good by promises of material reward. Wise men study philosophy, not so they will remain young forever, but that they may grow old wisely. No man studies the Ancient Wisdom teachings with a view to increasing his personal wealth, because philosophy, if anything, will probably separate him from what he now has. Philosophy makes men rich not in outward possessions but in inward consciousness. Philosophy stores up treasures within, where thieves cannot steal nor time corrupt. Jesus did not teach a doctrine of wealth and prosperity. He bade those who would be his disciples to leave what they had and come with him. It is written of the Christian Master that the foxes had holes and the birds had nests, but the Son of Man had no place to lay his head. Buddha left wealth behind and journeyed up and down the Indian road with beggar's bowl. Mohammed sacrificed a fortune and became a hunted wanderer without wood for a fire or enough food to eat. He wove his own clothes and pegged his own shoes.

The philosopher lives to give to others, and to bring joy to others and to serve others, retaining less and less for himself. How different is this glorious impersonal vision from the distorted picture of hundreds of foolish people listening frantically to metaphysical platitudes, in the hope that this listening will add a few dollars to their income. The whole picture is just wrong. The words of the great are misquoted. Fraudulent teachers try to picture Jesus as teaching a doctrine of prosperity, the Eastern saints as inviting the foolish to Nirvana. The law and the prophets are misquoted and mistranslated in an effort to make them justify the foolish belief that God wants all men to be healthy, happy and rich, whether they live well or not. As a matter of fact, the universe has no particular interest in man's happiness, any more than man is moved deeply by the state of comfort or discomfort that may exist in a beehive or ant-hill. In nature, man is simply a troublesome bi-ped, of distinctly destructive tendencies, living off the toil and life of others.

In order to be happy, man must live well. He must be honest to his world, honest to himself, and conscious of the purpose for his own existence. If man keeps the laws of life, lives intelligently and nobly, and uses his mind for the perfection of his inward nature and for the assistance of others, he is entitled to a reasonable amount of happiness. In fact, if he does these things, he is happy and is not spending his time looking around for platitudinous solutions to his imperfections. The same principle applies to the problem of wealth. Nature has not decreed nor the universe foreordained that man should be wealthy, in fact the whole theory of wealth is of human fabrication, for nature stores up what it needs and man accumulates what he does not need. If the law of Karma brings wealth to an individual, it becomes a problem in opportunity and responsibility. The prophets of old and the great World Teachers were certainly far too wise to advocate a program of universal wealth. Wealth is the heaviest responsibility that an individual has to carry in this world, and right decision concerning its use is one of the heaviest causes of Karma. It is a constant temptation and binds the individual to a host of responsibilities and decisions. It takes up a vast amount of time and renders the mind confused and wearied and unfitted for philosophical study. So, the possession of it is certainly no fundamental requisite of metaphysics. Those who have earned it for this life, by the law of Karma, have it. Whether they continue to have it or not after this life depends upon the use they make of it. As Buddha so wisely observed, the misuse of wealth must inevitably result in poverty in the future life. True metaphysics is concerned with universal facts, with the divine life of man that extends far beyond this mortal sphere.

True metaphysics is life under law, man flowing through the universe upon the currents of divine law like a ship moved by the great currents of the ocean. The wise man does not desire to escape from law but rather aspires to perfect harmony with it. There is a beautiful sentiment in the words of Confucius relating to this mystery. "Fishes," said the Chinese sage, "are born in the water. Man is born in the law. If fishes find ponds they thrive; if a man lives in the law, he may live his life in peace." Any metaphysical teacher, therefore, who would tempt man's mind away from the acceptance of those universal principles which sustain the world is guilty of the promulgation of false doctrines.

Metaphysics, like all the great branches of learning, has its own tradition and its own descent through a sequence of enlightened teachers. The great doctrines of metaphysics are all thoroughly established, and no important change or reform of the principles is likely or possible. Metaphysicians of today are not wiser than Lao Tze, more able than Plato, or more profound than Shankaracharya. It is a foolish man indeed who would attempt to reform the wisdom of the ages when he cannot reform the foolishness and error of the present generation. A student who desires a firm foundation in the principles of metaphysics cannot do better than to make part of his life the seven requisites of perfection established by the initiate philosophers of India. The statement of the seven requisites is given under the collective title of the paramitas. These are the rules and regulations of personal conduct indispensable to the mystical or philosophic life. Three different orders of paramitas are to be found in different teachings, arising from the same root. In one order there are six regulations, in another ten, but the order of seven most clearly sets forth the required virtues which must precede enlightenment in any legitimate metaphysical system.

The seven paramitas are as follows:

1. DANA, which means charity, a word which infers the whole philosophy of giving, serving and sharing. Without charity, there can be no virtue, without virtue there can be no wisdom, and without wisdom there can be no inward life. DANA is therefore the administration of social relationships, the overcoming of the error of the possessive urge, the real fundamental and honest desire to be of assistance to the needs of mankind. Charity is not only in physical things but in thoughts and opinions. We must not only give of what we have but of what we are. Charity is the overcoming of prejudices, the establishment of the realization of common purpose, common need, and common good. This might seem far remote from a metaphysical doctrine, but all inward development must, to a considerable degree, be influenced by the concepts and attitudes of the outer life.

2. SHILA. This word is variously interpreted to mean either harmony, obedience, or the keeping of the precepts, that is, the various regulations of virtuous conduct. Harmony is inward peace arising from realization, from obedience to the laws of life, and from the keeping of the philosophical precepts. Harmony is the beautifying of action, the invoking of an entirely constructive and cooperative mood. The thought may be summed up in the Western statement that he who lives the life shall know the doctrine. Without harmony, there can be no sensitiveness to superphysical realizations. Without obedience there can be no organization of the life into a pattern appropriate to the achievement of philosophical understanding. To keep the precepts means to obey the laws of life, for no man can outrage the universal dictums and be capable at the same time of understanding the secrets of life.

3. KSHANTI. This may be interpreted as either perseverance or patience. Perseverance is continuity of effort, the continuance of striving over a long period of time. Metaphysics is a science not easily mastered. Years and lives must be spent in unbroken effort if the great goal is finally to be attained. Patience is willingness to wait and without patience, the long process of perseverance cannot be finally consummated. Patience is not only willingness to wait, it is indifference in a sense to the time element in accomplishment. One must forget his hopes of illumination in six months or six years or sixty years, continue sincerely in his effort and realize that the reward

will come in due time. The workings of nature are not to be hastened by any desperate effort to accomplish everything here and now. Without patience, there can be no illumination, no consummation of effort. Metaphysics is the most profound form of human knowledge and the rewards of effort in this direction should not be envisioned as imminent. Man should never expect metaphysical enlightenment until he has perfected himself in every department of living and thinking.

4. VIRAG. This is interpreted as the higher indifference, detachment, the ability to release oneself from the striving of the senses, from all immoderations of aspiration or ambition, yes, even from the hope of the result or reward of effort. Obeying the law for its own sake, living nobly because it is the noble way to live, doing all things well without hope of reward or fear of loss, indifference to life, to time, to persons and to things—a complete release from the stress of striving—the hopes of success, fears of failure—all dispelled by a sustaining inward tranquility. Without detachment, there is no achievement. Philosophical indifference is not the type which neglects responsibility but does all things well, at the same time not permitting the doing or the things done to disturb the tranquility of the inward sense.

5. VIRYA. This may be interpreted as either effort rightly directed, or courage wisely administered. Really the thought is effort or striving without effort—a subtle Eastern metaphysical distinction. The doing of the thing is smoothly and subtly performed. All courage is directed towards the overcoming of the obstacles between the present state and the final illumination, the courage to renounce all lesser things in the cause of the greater, the courage to face danger, ridicule, criticism and even martyrdom with perfect poise, the mind fixed on the ultimate goal. Striving, in Eastern thought, is not a desperate running around or a panting after power. It is a gentle but inevitable force, never acknowledging defeat, moving slowly and certainly, beautifully and virtuously towards enlightenment.

6. DHYANA. This is contemplation, meditation, the inward envisioning of the goal of effort, the retiring of the objective into the subjective. At this point, the disciplines become esoteric. Dhyana is man's subjective union with the Law. Through the practice of it, the individual merges himself with universals. The true significance of the meditative process is not often understandable to those who have not already thoroughly practiced the preceding Paramitas. Dhyana is the practicing of the inward life, the silent realization by which man is finally instructed in the great universal truths, by these very truths themselves, which flow in upon him and fill him with

the Law itself.

7. PRAJNA. This is the last of the paramitas and is variously interpreted as either wisdom or the capacity for subjective perception. It consummates the processes and through the practice of Prajna wisdom, in the sense of the eternal truths of being, is finally attained. The quest ends in truth and the Law. Individuality is submerged, personality is eliminated as a philosophical factor. Universality alone continues.

The paramitas begin in simple, physical virtue, and end in transcendent metaphysical accomplishment.

The preceding outline, while subject to minor variations in different metaphysical systems, is the inevitable formula in every sincere and honest metaphysical or mystical school. There has never been any of the great Mystery Schools that ever-promised power, enlightenment or security until after the individual perfected the virtues within himself. It must be evident that a group of people gathered from all parts of a community, with no effort made to discriminate between their varying degrees of undevelopment, can never be promised any spiritual advantage by any metaphysical teacher or organization. Metaphysics is all inward chemistry, philosophical chemistry, based on the principle, the better we are, the more we can know. If we are not anything in ourselves, it is humanly impossible for any being, human or divine, to impress upon us the realization of truths beyond the state of our own development. There is no exception to this, there is no way of avoiding, evading or escaping this fundamental metaphysical fact.

Any effort to force conditions which are not merited comes under the heading of Black, Magic or sorcery. A sorcerer is simply a person who uses the mechanical processes of the will in an effort to force out of nature things or conditions not merited under the law of Karma. By hypnosis, by the exercise of will power, by formulas, it is sometimes possible to temporarily here in the physical world force the semblance of unjustified conditions. A man can steal by metaphysical means just the same as he might rob a bank or forge a name, or in some other harmful way come into possession of that which is not his own, but the mere fact that it can be accomplished in such a manner does not justify the process nor make right the wrong principle which is involved. By the malicious use of willpower and animal magnetism, the law of cause and effect can apparently be nullified for a short time. But again, the mere fact that it can be accomplished does not establish the integrity of such a process. The only way in which any individual can honestly possess what he desires is to earn or deserve that thing. Again, there are no exceptions. When some metaphysician stands up and tells you that he has a private way with the universe by which he can justify the misuse of power, only very foolish people will pay any attention to him. Black magic is not philosophy any more than bank robbery is ethics. If the whole problem is lifted to a metaphysical level, untrained minds are very apt to lose sight of values and proportions. Metaphysical black magic has flourished for many thousands of years, for there always has been and will probably continue to be for an indefinite period of time a class of people who desire to possess without the labor of acquiring by legitimate means. No one can be morally dishonest and at the same time pretend to be spiritual or philosophical.

On the other hand, it would be wrong to say that man's spiritual efforts, when wisely and honestly directed, are not rewarded in a wholly adequate way. The reason why most metaphysicians are not rewarded for their metaphysics is because they are following faulty and erroneous lines of thought and do not deserve reward. Men like Plato, Socrates, and Aristotle have been rewarded for their integrity not only by philosophical security during the periods of their lives, but by the generous praise of posterity that will remember their names and worlds until the end of time. Greatness may be obscured in its own day but it survives as a monument to itself and to those who achieve it. There were many brilliant men among the Athenians whose names have not survived to this century, because the measure of their achievement was too low to be regarded as a contribution to the eternal welfare of man. Politicians, diplomats, princes, the rich, the proud and the pompous who were important and revered in their own day find no place in the memory of man. The ages sought out values. That which is real ultimately receives the approbation of the race. Thus, we may say that wisdom bestows security upon the individual while he lives, protects him in the invisible world to which he goes, and bestows immortality upon his name in the world which he leaves behind. What more can the reasonably minded person desire than that the good things he does shall live after him, to deserve and receive the gratitude of humanity? Wisdom bestows a security far beyond that of wealth, gives inward peace and outward patience. It clears the mind of innumerable false values that clutter up the reasoning of the majority, it frees thought to contemplate the real. Philosophy rewards men with a coinage of its own, it gives them that which they have earned and which the world cannot take from them. Wisdom is its own reward and those who possess it can never be humiliated, impoverished or degraded. Wisdom is not of this world but of the secret world that lies behind. The rewards of wisdom are not of this world but also of that secret place, which is the abode of wisdom. Wise men retire from worldliness to dwell in the presence of truth and, in this, achieve the rational end for which the human fabric was devised.

Hence we cannot say that the quest for truth is all struggle and no result, for with each small gain we make within ourselves there is an appropriate extension of consciousness and enlightenment in our natures. The only thing is that we must learn not to think of philosophy in terms of dollars and cents, of real estate and of mortgages. Philosophy does not pay us in dollars because they are not of the world of philosophy. Man has an erroneous idea that by unfolding consciousness, he can become one of the princes of the earth, possessing all material things and an object of universal admiration. If a man wishes to improve his business, let him study not religion but business methods. There are institutions all over the country to fit men for greater efficiency in their various industrial, economic and commercial lines. One does not study philosophy to become a salesman, one studies salesmanship. The things which belong intrinsically to the material universe should be mastered on the material plane, with material force and material means. Religion is not super-salesmanship, nor is it a substitute for the doctor, the dentist and the grocer. The work of religion is to give man inner character, not outer opulence. It often follows that man's material conditions are improved by his religion, but it also frequently follows that materially he remains an insignificant figure. It is a terrible mistake to use spiritual means in an effort to accomplish material ends. It is a distinct prostitution of that which is too fine and too noble to be so perverted and contaminated. The honest-minded metaphysician should avoid, as he would the plague, teachers and teachings which promise him freedom from the physical responsibilities of life and the famous "peace, power and plenty" psychology of the inflated 20's.

It has been our sincere desire in the preparation of these letters to bring to you a practical summary of the problems of the spiritual life, particularly as these problems affect the beginner who must seek for truth through one of those jarring sects that make up the metaphysical-religious field of today. It may be a disappointment to some to realize that religion as aphorism or platitude is not a substitute for living, wording and thinking, but this discovery must finally be made, and once made, becomes the guiding star in the quest for real and permanent values.

If we could only restore some of the dignity and the beauty of ancient religion. If we could only bring back that olden day when the great philosophers and their disciples wandered the roads of the world, teaching the glories of the universe and the wonders of the inner self. Gone are the noble masters of that elder day. Only their shadows have descended to us, a few fragments of their words, a story, a fable. These alone bind us to the great philosophical institutions of the past. We live in a material generation and our minds have become used to the idea of interpreting everything on a cash basis. The abstract wealth of beauty, of dream, of vision, of hope and aspiration, of ethics and logic—all this is beyond the appreciation of the average man of today. We must interpret all knowledge into the productive channels of industry or else that knowledge seems very remote, abstract and impractical. The underlying materialistic psychology of the age contributes much to religious fraud. We attempt to establish our theologies on the profit system. Confused by the standards of this generation, we even try to make money-lenders of our sages and exploiters of our prophets. We induce ourselves to believe that the Pythagoreans were pioneers in the field of super-salesmanship, and that the Eastern sages and the Western philosophers were all desperately concerned with distributing prosperity among the uninformed.

We must build towards a nobler interpretation of our faiths or else prepare to see our beliefs crumble with the decadency of our economics. The whole world today is envisioning a period to come when money will not be the sovereign factor in our thoughts and lives. We are beginning to realize the limitations of wealth and that money is only useful to the degree that it can contribute to our opportunity to improve our inward selves. Today, money can secure leisure but cannot guarantee the intelligent use of leisure. It can purchase education, but education is bankrupt as far as ethical and esthetic values are concerned. What all men are really seeking is some form of inner contentment or tranquility that can give them courage over outer circumstances. Philosophy bestows the strength of right decision, it gives resistance to temptation, and leveling all extremes of action, reduces wealth and poverty to a common state, elevating only truth to a position of first importance. We all desire to be better than we are. There are millions of people in this country who want to understand the principles of the mystic life. In their hearts, these people are willing, but their viewpoints are distorted by false teachings and inadequate understanding. To these people must come the realization that honesty is the beginning of wisdom and that without honesty, no great spirituality can be accomplished. Honesty should have its beginning in the realization that we have no right to anything we have not earned. Also, that if by any chance we temporarily secure through the accidents of the material life something that is not rightly our own by merit, the final loss of this possession is inevitable. What we have, we must use wisely, what we have not, we must earn. All the theological prayers of the ages put together have not the constructive power of one nobly executed action or one profoundly realized truth. To pray for things, we have not earned is dishonest; to pray to be relieved of evils we have not mastered is dishonest; to desire anything that is not merited is unphilosophical.

We may be in doubt as to which cult to belong, and we may be in doubt as to which teacher we should follow. The competition of creeds may leave us upon the horns of a dilemma, but of one thing we can be sure, regardless of our creeds or our beliefs—the spiritual life begins with right action. Honesty is the first step towards truth. Self-control, inward tranquility, detachment from possession, balance of emotion—all these virtues are absolutely necessary to the understanding of any religious or philosophical system. So, if you are in doubt as to which god to worship or which philosophy to study, do not decide on such issues immediately. First put your life in order and the foundation of right living will give you the discrimination to choose your beliefs honestly and intelligently.

Yours sincerely,

Manly P. Hall

AUTHOR AND MANAGING EDITOR

Darrell Jordan is an acolyte of the August Fraternity, former Noble Grand-IOOF and Freemason. He is also a member of the Theosophical and Philalethes Societies.

Darrell Jordan

BOOKS BY THE AUTHOR

- Illustrations of Masonry
- Surviving Document of the Widow's Son
- The Undiscovered Teachings of Jesus
- The Initiates
- Jefferson's Bible
- Master Masons Handbook
- Forgotten Essays - W.L. Wilmshurst
- Forgotten Essays - Waite
- Forgotten Essays - H. Stanley Redgrove
- The Writings of Sigismond Bacstrom M.D.
- Forgotten Essays – Reincarnation
- Masonic Writings of George Oliver
- Masonic Lectures by Wellins Calcott
- The Fellowcraft Handbook
- Secret Societies
- Vibration and Life
- Key to the Rosicrucian Characters
- The Revelation of John
- Life and the Ideal
- The Philosophical History of Freemasonry
- The Magic of the Middle Ages
- Musings of a Chinese Mystic
- The Life of the Soul
- Christian Mysticism
- Krishna and Orpheus
- The Eleusinian Mysteries & Rites
- The Crucifixion Letter
- The Mystic Key
- You Paid What?
- The Illustrated Pioneer History of the America
- Montana Freemasons 19th Century
- Washington Freemasons 19th Century
- Idaho Freemasons 19th Century
- Rock Metaphysics
- Emblems: Jean Jacque Boissard and Otto van Veen
- Emblems: Nicholas M. Meerfeldt
- Alchemy Art: Manly P. Hall
- Emblems: Manly P. Hall
- Alchemy Art & Symbols
- Splendor Solis

For the latest information, please visit author's book site:

Parallel47North.com/collections/esoteric-books

If you have any question, suggestion, or feedback, please contact:

info@Parallel47North.com

Books by the Author

MANLY P. HALL BOOK SERIES

All Seeing Eye Book Series

A Seeker of More Intelligent Life Book Series

Hand-drawn Illustration of Manly P. Hall and Book Cover Art by Jessica Naomi.

The Artist Portfolio: JessicaNaomiDesigns.com

www.ingramcontent.com/pod-product-compliance
Lightning Source LLC
Chambersburg PA
CBHW020309010526
44107CB00001B/46